Diwan-e-Ghalib
(A Selection)

r

DIWAN-e-GHALIB

(A Selection)

Selection and English Translation by
Kuldip Salil

rajpal

Price : Rs. 175.00 (Rupees One Hundred Seventy Five)

Edition : 2009 © Kuldip Salil
ISBN : 978-81-7028-692-9
Diwan-e-Ghalib Translated by Kuldip Salil

RAJPAL & SONS
Madarsa Road, Kashmere Gate, Delhi-110 006
website : www.rajpalpublishing.com
e-mail : mail@rajpalpublishing.com

Preface

Although Ghalib has been a part of my growing up from early boyhood, the idea of translating him is not more than a year old. I must confess that when the suggestion first came from a friend, I had serious trepidation. But once I started the work I experienced little difficulty. In fact, I took more time in writing the 'Introduction' than in translating the ghazals. This was perhaps because I have been for many years now translating poetry from Hindi and Urdu into English and vice-versa, my first translation work being Shamsher Bahadur Singh's Sahitya Academy award-winning collection of poems from Hindi into English. A collection of my translation of some of the best-known English poems from Shakespeare to W.H. Auden was published two years back.

Translating Ghalib was, however a different proposition altogether. For one thing, translating a ghazal into English and still retaining its charm and appeal is, indeed, difficult. And in the case of Ghalib, this difficulty is even greater. It is relatively easy to give prose translation of a ghazal. It may serve some purpose but conveys little of the charm and beauty of the original. In fact, it is well-nigh impossible to do full justice to poetry, particularly the ghazal in translation. The best I thought that could be done was to translate the verses into independent rhymed couplets. Also, I have tried to be faithful to the original. I have not attempted to translate the entire Diwan-e-Ghalib; I could'nt have. It is only a selection from the Urdu Dewan.

In my assessment of Ghalib's poetry in the 'Introduction', I have given some of its traits that I have long thought make him a great poet. I have also given illustrations from the text.

In writing about the life and times of the poet, I have drawn on many sources. Among them are the works of Quratulain Hyder, Ijaz Ahmed, Ralph Russel, Pavan Varma and Sardar Jafri. I express my gratitude to these learned authors. I would, in this regard, acknowledge my debt particularly to Ralph Russel. I have greatly benefitted from his scholarly work. Hali's 'Yadgar-e-Ghalib' has of course been a primary source.

I would like to express my thanks to Dr. Khalid Ashraf of the Department of Urdu, Kirori Mal College and to Dr. S.R. Singh, Dr. C.D. Verma, Professor S.N. Sharma, Professor K.G. Verma and Mithuraaj Dhusiya at the department of English of Delhi University and Mr. O.P. Sapra for their valuable help and suggestions, and for reading through the manuscript. Dr. Khalid, in fact, settled for me the meaning of some of the controversial verses. Thanks are also due to my daughters Ritu and Sarika for their help in preparing the manuscript. I express my thanks also to Shri Vishv Nath who suggested the project to me and encouraged me at every step.

—Kuldip Salil
1770. Outram Line,
Kingsway Camp,
Delhi-110009

Introduction

Mirza Asad-Ullah Khan Ghalib is the greatest Urdu poet, and one of the greatest in any Indian language. He could rank perhaps among the great poets of the world. There is an intersting parallel between Meer Taqi Meer and Mirza Ghalib on the one hand, and William Shakespeare and John Milton on the other. Shakespeare died in 1616 when Milton was eight years old. Ghalib was about Milton's age when Meer, who was then in his last days, read some of Ghalib's writings, which were taken to him by an early admirer of Ghalib. And if Shakespeare and Milton are the greatest English poets, Meer and Ghalib are the greatest in Urdu. There is one difference though—in English it is the senior poet who is the greatest, in Urdu it is the junior.

With Meer, Ghalib, Iqbal and Faiz, to name only four, the firmament of Urdu poetry is truly star-studded, with numerous starlets strewn around. Ghalib has not only a pride of place among them; his stature is growing with every passing decade. He got less than his due in his own time. He was ahead of his age, and his contemporaries failed to comprehend him fully. Then he was pilloried on conventional moral grounds. Add to these his difficult language and subtlety of thought. As a result, his reputation as a poet suffered not only in his own day, but for decades after his death. In this respect, his friend and disciple, Altaf Hussain Hali with his 'Yadgar-e-Ghalib' rendered yeoman's service in establishing him. Others too saw his merit as a poet, but it was really when India (and Pakistan) celebrated his first death centenary in 1969 that he was rehabilitated as a great poet that he is. There has been no looking back after that. As with other great poets like Shakespeare, one discovers a new wealth of meaning every time one reads him, and different people find different meaning, suiting their need and situation. In other words, great poets are inexhaustible in their appeal and meaning and do not get dated even when they mirror their times most effectively. Ghalib's writings are not only an authentic account of his own age, his poetry transcends his times and situation. It is universal in its appeal.

Ghalib is truly a modern poet. Modern age is characterised by doubt and scepticism, irony and satire, suggestiveness and understatement, a rational outlook (at least professedly), a result oriented scientific attitude and secularism. When asked by Sir Sayyed Ahmed Khan to write a preface to his edited version of 'Aaeen-e-Akbari', Ghalib wrote it in verse, praising Sir Sayyed in the beginning but lambasting him for his efforts to flog a dead horse, pointing out that rather than eulogising Akbar's administration, one would do well to learn from modern scientific inventions and works being undertaken by the British— things like steam-ships, railways, telegraph—and their streamlined administration and discipline. His dictum was—*murda parvardan mubarak kaar-neest*—(there is no credit in praising the dead ideals.)

Sir Sayyed felt so annoyed that he did not use Ghalib's preface.

One of the factors in Ghalib's greatness is his ability to detach himself from himself. He was afflicted by a whole lot of troubles, his life was a veritable tale of woe, and yet, he is able to laugh at himself. He was jailed for defaulting on payment to the moneylender. After his release, Ghalib agreed to stay at one Kale Sahib's house. Says he, "Which bastard says that I have been released from jail? Earlier I was in white man's jail, now I am in black man's custody." When a friend paid the fine for the default in payment because Ghalib was in no position to pay, the poet writes.

We drank on credit, but always knew
That our recklessness will one day a mischief do

Ghalib separates himself from his suffering, looks at them bemused from a distance, brings out their poignancy, presents them most effectively—and jokes about them. He can speak about his humiliations, his misdeeds, his sorrows most objectively as if they were not his own but those of somebody else. And thus perhaps make them bearable :

> *Ghalib would be torn to pieces, the news was hot*
> *We too went to witness the fun, but it was not*

He can cast a cold glance at his own situation, be merciless and lambast himself :

How could you have, the cheek, Ghalib to do, a pilgrimage
to Kaba.
But Shame is perhaps the last thing to have touched you

An outstanding feature of Ghalib's poetry and prose is his wit and humour, often at his own cost:

> *You are his liege Ghalib, so bless the King*
> *Gone are the days when you could say you 're not serving*

Wit, humour, irony and satire sum up the sunny side of Ghalib's personality. When somebody said that if he continued drinking, his prayers will not be granted by God, Ghalib retorted that if somebody gets wine to drink, what does he need to pray for. He was a courteous man. Once he carried a candle to help a friend find his shoes. When the friend protested, Ghalib replied that he was doing so to make sure that "you do not take away my shoes." And his famous jibe on Zauq apparently at his own cost can amuse us for even and ever.

> *But a king's courtier he struts up and down*
> *Otherwise who cares for Ghalib in the town.*

This wit and humour is a strong shield against sufferings. In fact a sturdiness of mind, even a stubbornness in the face of sufferings that emerges from his writings is a great thing about Ghalib. It is noteworthy that misfortunes cannot crush his spirits. His zest, even lust for life is unlimited.'

> *My hands are lifeless though, my eyes are still bright*
> *Remove not the cup and the bottle yet from my sight.*

If misfortunes cannot crush his spirits, they cannot curb his generosity either. Ghalib was a very compassionate man. Once he found a friend wearing a coat that was in tatters. Meeting him next time, he says "Lovely coat! I like it. Can you exchange it for mine?" So saying, he took off his own new coat and gave it to him.

This joviality enables him to retain his sanity in the midst of troubles. His is a great example of defiant and cheerful stoicism; he attempts to transmute personal sorrow into a joyous splendour of agony. He is in a large part a romantic poet, but none of the English romantic poets for instance—except Byron, perhaps—shows the doughty sense of humour that Ghalib possesses. Even W.B. Yeats, the greatest English poet of the twentieth century could acquire this ability to be amused at his own predicament, to stand detached from it only in his later poetry.

Ghalib is a poet of human sufferings; he may even be called a tragic poet. Sufferings are an essential truth of life :

> *Life's suffering has no end, Asad, except demise*
> *The candle burns in any case till the dawn*
> *arrives.*
>
> *or*
>
> *Life's incarceration and bondage to suffering*
> *are the same thing indeed*
> *Until our death, how can we from suffering be relieved*

He writes a full elegy on the death of his nephew, Arif:

> *A full waxing moon for my house you were*
> *Then why could you not shine a little longer!*

Ghalib's letters and poetry present a moving picture of his times in the aftermath of the revolt of 1857 and its terrible failure. In letter after letter he narrates incidents and instances of massive suffering that befell the people of Delhi, people that included his close friends and relations, acquaintances and general population. His account of how families were devastated, how children died for want of milk and food, how the helpless and poor suffered, how people were driven mad because of their sorrow, has a poignancy which no history book could convey.

It is more effective than any historical account because it is an account of events personally experienced and most feelingly conveyed. And his ghazals distil the essence of these times.

Ghalib's poetry, however, reflects not on his times only but the human situation in general:

In the case of the heart, how can you avoid grief though it is life consuming
If it were not the grief of love, it would have been the travail of earning a living

or

To fade away from the world O Ghalib, is all I desire
Its manner of hospitality has set me on fire

And he has no illusion about himself:

What business of life without Ghalib the miserable has shut its door
Why should anybody cry his heart out if he is no more

In fact he is totally free from illusions. Even about heaven he has none:

Though we know full well the truth about heaven
As a surmise Ghalib it is a good one

This is in keeping with his rational outlook. Though he has no illusion about himself, it does not mean that he does not know his worth; he knows it too well:

In our case, it is the gallows
and the hangman's noose that are on test
Farhad and Qais were tested at their best.
By the stature and tresses of their beloveds,

He is quite conscious of his uniqueness :

It is not our wont to flow through the veins
How is it blood, if not from the eyes it rains.

Even with God, he wants reciprocity. Says Ghalib :

Such is my sense of self respect that even though I went
to pray
If the doors of Kaba were not open, I came away.

For him, serving the beloved is alright - in fact he would be very glad to serve her - but humiliation is not :

She will not change her attitude,
then why should my ways be changed
Why humiliate myself and ask her why she is estranged

He is willing to go through the hardest test to prove his worth and feels let down when ignored. He lays great store by his poetry and passion. He thinks he is with Qais and Farhad and perhaps more devoted than they, and is capable of equaling (or exceling) Christ and Sikandar:

Solomon's throne for me is only a plaything
And Christ's miracle an ordinary something

But even while he knows his own stature as a man and a poet, he is quite willing to acknowledge the greatness of others :

There was they say, in the olden days a certain Meer too
You alone are not the master, Ghalib, of the poetry in Urdu

Like Meer, Ghalib had a high sense of self respect. He would not visit people who did not return his first visit. A classic example of this self-regard is his turning down of a teaching job at Delhi College even though in those days he was living in dire poverty. He was offered a professorship in Persian. He went in a palinquin and waited at the gate of the college. After a while, he asks the palinquin bearers to return home. The reason—the principal of the college had not come to the gate to receive him. The poor principal waited in his office.

There is a restlessness and a creative energy in Ghalib, struggling for expression and recognition. Again and again he gives expression to the impediments that he faces in the pursuit of his goal and his confidence in his powers:

As I went to the garden, it began with verse and melody to ring
For, the nightingales, as they heard my song, began to sing

In a way, Ghalib is a poet of conflict. Great literature comes to grips with paradoxes of life, the inherent contradictions in the human situation, and the conflicts both within and outside.'

> *Truth pulls at me as falsehood attractive I find.*
> *The cathedral is in my front, the Kaba behind*

He lived in a period when the old culture and its values were facing extinction and a new era was taking birth. He is also a poet of dilemmas, general and personal.

> *We expect faithfulness from those in return*
> *Who know not what it is, have no concern*
> *Or*
> *Desire is impatient and love much patience needs*

However, even though he was a man of the old culture, he had no hesitation in embracing the new and the upcoming.

Ghalib was one of the most secular poets we know of. He never kept the more troublesome commandments of religion. He did not say the five daily prayers, did not keep the Ramzan fasts, had no great ambition to make a pilgrimage to Mecca and broke with a vengeance the Islamic prohibition on wine. As Hali says "From the duties of worship and the enjoined practices of Islam, he took only two — a belief that God is one and immanent in all things, and a love for the prophet and his family. And this alone he considered sufficient for salvation. Once at the end of the Ramzan fast the King asked him, "Mirza, how many days' fast did you keep?" Ghalib replied, "My Lord and guide. I failed to keep one," leaving it for the King to decide whether he failed to keep only one or any at all.

Of the two dominant currents in Islamic thought—fundamentalism and Sufism—Ghalib subscribed to the latter. While the former is preached and practised by the mullahs, Sufism is liberal and all-embracing. Its best examples are Amir Khusro and Nizam-u-din Aulia. It is no coincidence that most of these Sufis were poets as well, who carried the message of universal love in their poetry and teachings. Their followers included both Hindus and Muslims.

Sufis were by and large, anti-establishment; they were rebels against the constricting social practices and prejudices, sectarianism and superstitions, ritualism and exploitation. Ghalib was in line with them. In his typical humorous way he could say even about paradise that the very idea of going there will terrify him; there will be infinite monotony, everlasting boredom—the same old emerald mansion, the same old branch of heavenly tree, the same old hoors.

His appreciation and respect for other religions is most eloquently expressed in 'Chiragh-e-Dair' (The Temple lamp) a poem in Persian that he wrote about Banaras. Nobody could praise Banaras more than Ghalib does in this poem. It is a grand eulogy on Hindu rituals and traditions and a great tribute to Hindu way of life. He calls Banaras the Kaba of Hind. Only a man of a Ghalib's secular and modern outlook could have written such a poem in those days.

Ghalib says that as he was not fortunate enough to be a soldier, he would have liked to be a darvesh or live a life of freedom. "But the love of poetry which I had brought with me from eternity assailed me and won my soul. I launched my ship on this illusory sea of verse. My pen became my banner, and the broken arrow of my ancestors became my pen."

Ghalib is not a political poet in the modern sense of the word—commitment to strategies of change and resistance. But surrounded by constant carnage, he wrote poetry of losses and grief. In sensibility, it is poetry, meditative and full of reverberations, couched in a language at once sparkling and fastidious. He wrote in a world that was becoming increasingly unbearable for a man of his sensibility.

Politically speaking, Ghalib is no rebel. He in fact for all his sympathy for the suffering fellow countrymen, was not a supporter of the revolt of 1857. However, as far as the strict moral and social code is concerned and in matters religious, he is an incorrigible rebel. He goes against the accepted feudal norms in love and the religious prohibition against drinking. Urdu and Persian poets have traditionally ridiculed the mullahs and maulvis, zahid and naseh, and even Khuda. Vagrancy, unshackled love, drinking, roaming in the jungles as a mark of protest against the prevailing social and moral code, have always been a stock in trade with these poets. Ghalib is in the forefront of this poetic tradition. He was fond of drinking, even gambling.

One of the traits of good poetry is that it liberates. It casts a spell on you, when you forget all trivialities, when you almost melt. It has a cathartic effect:

What shapes and forms must lie buried in dust
Not all, but only a few in the form of flowers burst
or
If Ghalib keeps weeping like this, 0 people of the world
You will soon see these towns into wilderness hurled

Sometime the poet is in a mood of self-abnegation; he juxtaposes himself against the mighty world and the impersonal universe, and shows his miniscule place in it. It is not always that the poet is pitting himself and challenging them. His stoicism, his speculations make us wonder at the mystery that is life and brings home to us the huge waste of great human material that is the fate of the world. Some of Ghalib's couplets are extremely moving:

He so lifted Asad's corpse yesterday
That even his enemies could not their tears stay

Ghalib is easily the most quotable of Urdu poets. There is not a mood or occasion for which he does not have a couplet:

He comes to our house, God shows his grace.
Sometime we look at him sometime at our place
or
However much we may discourse on the true and divine
It'll be incomplete unless we bring in the cup and the
wine

He gives the impression of a man who has not only experienced and observed life most intensely, but who has thought long and hard on it. He can be philosophic and can distil the highest wisdom of all scriptures in couplets like:

❧ 15 ❧

The world for me is but a children's playground
Where night and day a funny something is happening around

If detachment is a great religious virtue, here it is. In fact religion, philosophy and poetry at their best are one.

II

Ghalib belonged to a family of soldiers of Turkish origin, who had migrated to India from Samarkand. He was extremely proud of his ancestory, which he claimed had a tradition of soldiering for a hundred generations. His grandfather had served under Emperor Shah Alam, and was killed in action. Ghalib regretted the fact that he broke with the family tradition of soldiering; and he was the first to do that.

Ghalib was born in December, 1797, in Agra and spent his early boyhood there. All his life he had fond memories of the city. He lived in Agra until the age of thirteen when he was married prematurely to a girl of eleven. After that he left Agra to live permanently in Delhi. Ghalib was left fatherless at the age of five and lived through the rest of his boyhood at the generosity of others. After the death of his father, Ghali'ɔ and the rest of the family became dependent on his maternal grandparents. His father had married in one of the most distinguished families of Agra. He had never set up a household of his own, and made his home with his wife's parents. His three children—two sons and a daughter—all grew up there.

This situation of dependence was prolonged by Ghalib's marriage in a family of Delhi, much wealthier than his own. In view of the aristocratic values of those days, his in-laws considered him as belonging to an inferior class. Ghalib, the intelligent and the sensitive boy that he was, felt all this very keenly. He lived in a family of which he was never an integral part. He learnt quite early in life to live aloof. "This, together with his intellectual sharpness produced a quality of ironic scepticism and a sense of humour, which both enhanced his capacity to enjoy life and armed it against its more bitter experiences". He understood the meaning of mental and emotional stress even when he was so young.

As Ghalib himself says, he was in love with a domni, a singing and a dancing girl. She died rather young. Forty years later, he spoke of the grief he experienced over her death : **"The memory of her charming ways comes back to me, and I shall not forget her or deny as I live."** But in his typical Ghalib vein, he goes on to advise a friend who had suffered a similar fate, **"Yet though grief tore at my soul and the pain of parting crushed the heart, we must strive to find the balm that can banish the distress. A man must in the midst of sorrow set out to learn the lesson of fortitude. A man should let the world of fragrance and colour win his heart, not bind it in the shackle of one love."** Notwithstanding all this, this girl became a fixation with him and he wrote numberless verses with her in his mind. Nothing seems to inspire his poetic impulse as she does in various moods of cruelty, rudeness, sorrow, and coquettery. She must obviously have been a woman of rare beauty and endowments.

Ghalib's grounding in Logic, Astronomy, Metaphysics, Medicine and the traditional sciences was strong. However his own inclination was towards literature, linguistics and Persian. Luckily for him an eminent scholar of Persian and Arabic, Abdus Samad visited Agra and stayed at Ghalib's house for two years. Ghalib became his pupil. If anybody can be called Ghalib's ustad, it was Samad. Otherwise Ghalib did not acknowledge anybody as his ustad. Ghalib was also influenced by the abstract writings of the Persian poets. It was not surprising in view of his inclinations towards metaphysics and philosophy.

From 1730 to 1803, Delhi had witnessed unprecedented anarchy and bloodshed. Its population of two millions in the days of emperor Aurangzeb was reduced to about one tenth of that number. It was only when the city came in the hands of the British, who systematically suppressed lawlessness, chaos and brigandage that some order was restored and life and property in the city became secure. In the ensuing half century of internal order and peace, Delhi experienced a kind of a renaissance and a flowering of literature and learning. Mughal culture and English culture met in these fifty years on terms of equality and mutual respect. Such a setting was most conducive to a man of Ghalib's background and learning. He took his place among Delhi's aristocracy, meeting them on equal footing and living in the same style and at the same level as they did. He zealously maintained a sense of self-respect. He never went out except in a palinquin. He would never call upon the nobles who did not visit him, and never failed to return the visits of those who did. He was fully involved also in the intellectual life of the city, which was then dominated by the controversies between traditional and rational school of Islamic thoughts.

Ghalib however remained uninvolved in these controversies. In fact his attitude towards religion was one of cheerful irreverence. Open and veiled criticism of God is common both in his poetry and prose. He shared the view expressed by Persian and Urdu poets long before him that man is a helpless puppet in the hands of God, he cannot do anything of his own volition and yet he is accused by God of being free and hence accountable to Him for his sins. Such sentiments are usually expressed humorously in Ghalib's writings. Again and again he takes jibes at the mullahs and the maulvis. He would not allow religion or the lack of it to become a cause of friction in personal relations with men, he otherwise liked.

Ghalib had a sharp intellect, which was accompanied by a phenomenal memory. He never, or practically never, bought a book. Instead, he would borrow a book, read it and never forget any striking idea or point of substance therein. His intellect, his prowess in Persian and his determination to be a poet of rare distinction led him to write in original but difficult style. As Hali says, he avoided ordinary form of expression. He was less concerned with making his verse easily intelligible than to write it in a striking and original way. Not surprisingly, his poetry came under criticism from the beginning. According to Hali the poets of Delhi would come to mushairas where Ghalib was present, and recited ghazals which looked impressive but were meaningless as though to tell Ghalib that this was the way he was writing. However, since Ghalib was a very intelligent person, he soon learnt his lesson from this criticism. In this, he was greatly helped by the criticism of Fazal-e-Haq Khairabadi, a man of learning for whom Ghalib had great regard. So much so, that when Ghalib compiled his Urdu divan, he discarded at Fazal-e-Haq's suggestion two third of all the Urdu ghazals he had written.

Thereafter without surrendering his originality, he tried to express what he had to say in more intelligible language. The controversies around his poetry, however were mostly not acrimonious because Ghalib was a very popular figure in Delhi. According to Hali, he was regarded as one of the most handsome men in the city—tall and well built with powerful limbs. He was a man to whom people got quickly attached. He had numerous friends from all communities and creeds. Also, he had a great reputation as an engaging conversationalist.

Except for the death of his heart throb, the singing and the dancing girl, the first half of Ghalib's life in Delhi had been a relatively happy one, until in a single year a series of misfortunes befell him. In 1826, his only bother Mirza Yusuf lost mental balance (and was to remain so for the rest of his life), his father-in-law died and he found himself in serious financial difficulties. His creditors were pressing him hard to repay his debts, which was just not possible for him to do. It is not difficult to understand why he found himself heavily in debt. He moved in the highest circle of Delhi society, and his pride would not allow him to live at a level much lower than that of his circle even though he just could not afford the expenses. Under these circumstances, Ghalib decided to approach the British authorities in Calcutta for 'pension' which was in fact a law suit against his half brother. For this purpose he set out for the then British capital in 1827 and was to stay away from Delhi for nearly three years. He failed to win his pension case, but gained in other ways. On way to Calcutta, he stayed for months at Lucknow and Banaras. The journey brought him in contact with men of letters in these and other cities, and he continued to maintain the contacts in years to come. Banaras particularly enchanted him and he wrote a Persian poem in praise of it 'Lamp of the

Temple.' And he continued to have fond memories of Calcutta. His famed love of mangoes alone would have endeared Calcutta to him. When a friend joked with him that even the donkeys don't like to eat mangoes, he retorted, "Only the donkeys don't."

Ghalib's debts at that time amounted to a huge Rs. 40,000 which was nearly sixty times his annual income. For a time, he kept to himself and avoided the society of others. Then two of his creditors took him to court. The court ordered him to pay Rs.5000 or go to jail. He, of course, had no means of paying. Fortunately, prominent men of Delhi were treated with special consideration and were not arrested so long as they kept to their own houses. So his imprisonment was no more than house-arrest. All the same this indignity rankled him greatly and he wrote of it bitterly to Nasikh, his poet friend in Lucknow. His losing the pension case had already made him a butt of ridicule among his detractors, and then these were by no means the only troubles he had.

In the midst of these hardships, Ghalib found comfort in writing and in his conviction that his greatness as a poet necessarily means living in the midst of misfortunes. It was during these years that he compiled the first volume of his Urdu ghazals. He also gathered together his Persian prose and poetry and wrote many new Persian ghazals.

Although writing comforted him, it did not lessen his financial worries. And he would not try to earn extra income in ways that he thought derogatory to his honour. Thus he missed the opportunity of a professorship in Persian in 1842.

Apart from drinking, Ghalib was fond of gambling, though he did not play for high stakes. His financial difficulties might have egged him on further in this direction. But now gambling had become rampant and a serious evil in Delhi and the authorities were determined to stamp it out. Ghalib's house was raided, he was arrested and sentenced to six month's rigorous imprisonment and a fine of two hundred rupees. This was a heavy blow because he could not understand how his influential contacts had failed to save him. The session judge, he says, "was my friend and behaved quite informally with me." This heavy sentence created quite a stir in Delhi. The king himself wrote to the authorities, but he received the reply that it was a matter for the court to decide. Unlike the earlier term, it was not an imprisonment at home and Ghalib had to go to jail.

This was most humiliating. And in these days of distress all his friends, except one, deserted him; some became even openly hostile. This one man was a fellow poet, Nawab Mustafa Khan Shefta. He paid all the expenses required for the trial from his own pocket, and as long as Ghalib was in jail, visited him regularly. Ghalib felt gratitude as intense for him as the bitterness he felt for his other fair weather friends.

However, Ghalib did not have to serve his full jail term or perform hard labour. Money was arranged to pay the fine, but he did spend three hard months in jail.

In 1850 the king's physician who was an admirer of Ghalib's Persian writings, got him a commission to write in Persian prose the history of the Mughal dynasty, for which he was to get an annual stipend of Rs. 600. Thus at the age of fifty one, he began to receive a regular income for the first time. Then in 1854 he was appointed the ustad of the heir apparent. In the same year Zauq died and Ghalib became King's ustad too. Thus at the end of 1854 his financial position was better than it had been for years. Besides his pension of Rs. 750 a year, he was getting Rs. 600 from the king, Rs. 400 from the heir apparent and Rs. 500 from the Nawab of Avadh.

The history of the Mughal dynasty was completed quickly in 1854, but as Ghalib himself says he did not feel inspired to write it. It was money alone that impelled him.

As far as poetry was concerned, his relations with the king were of an ambiguous and uneven kind. His rivalry with Zauq, the king's ustad is well known; one of the reasons for this was that Ghalib thought the kind of poetry Zauq and his followers were writing was an inferior example of poetry. Although Ghalib was not entirely right in this; he thought that much of Zafar's and Zauq's poetry, though polished, lacked depth, and that he could not admire verse which was just mediocre. According to Hali, there was no element of jealousy in it. One cannot be too sure. However one cannot accuse Hali of partisanship, because he himself thought that Zauq's and for that matter, Momin's poetry was of an inferior kind. Ghalib himself went to the mushairas with mixed feelings because he knew that much of the poetry recited there was of a poor kind.

With the passage of time, Ghalib had acquired a great reputation for poetry and had many disciples, who wanted both instructions and adulatory prefaces for their books. Ghalib could however be blunt in such cases. He seems to have annoyed even his friend Tufta in this respect. Very soon he discovered that the task of pleasing an author and at the same time expressing his own honest opinion about his work was a very difficult task.

Ghalib encouraged the same independence of judgement to his friends and disciples **"Pay no heed to what others see and feel but increase your own perception,"** he wrote to a friend. He was quite clear as to which poets deserved attention and among them he of course included himself. He was full of praise for the Persian poets. Among the Urdu poets, he had regards for Meer and Sauda. He was much delighted on meeting a man whose love of poetry and discrimination was as great as his own. However, he did not attempt to impose his own style on his shagirds. He could be frank even with the king. Hali narrates a number of incidents to show how freely Ghalib behaved even with his royal master. The same attitude is visible in his conversations and jokes about religion, though the king was religiously orthodox. When Ghalib recited:

This felicity of expression, these philosophical discourses great
Were you not a drinker Ghalib, you would have been divinity incarnate

the king said that he would not consider him a saint even if he did not drink. Ghalib replied "You consider me a saint even now, but you don't say so lest sainthood should go to my head."

It is to this period that many of the best known anecdotes relating to his attitude towards religion belong. When somebody for instance, lectured him against drinking and said that the prayers of the wine-drinkers are not granted, pat came Ghalib's reply "My friend, if a man has wine to drink, what does he pray for?"

Ghalib might or might not have foreseen the revolt of 1857, but he knew that the British were moving towards ending the Mughal power and when the revolt came, he was not in sympathy with it. It was so, not because of any loyalty to the British but because of his conviction that it was bound to fail and would bring a trail of misery in its wake. He was not only a great poet, he was a shrewd man of the world also and was keen to secure his future. He did not even condemn the excesses which the British committed, though he wrote bitterly of the execution of nawabs of three small states in the neighborhood of Delhi.

However the events of 1857 greatly affected his family. In this chaos and anarchy, he says he was living in anxious thoughts of providing bread and butter for himself and his family. To add to his problems, he had adopted two little boys from his wife's side, and having no surviving issue of his own, was very greatly attached to them. And then, his mad brother's family depended on him. This was an additional cause for worry. What grieved him most was the loss of many friends in the revolt. He had friends in all camps and all communities. "I hold all mankind as my kin and look upon Hindus, Muslims, Christians as my brothers" he says and adds "Alas, so many of my friends are dead that now if I die there will be no one to mourn for me."

He lived for about twelve years after the revolt, but the feeling of loneliness never quite left him. The British retook the city in September 1857 and immediately expelled most of the population.

While the Hindus were allowed to return after three months, the Muslims could come back only after two years. All the time Ghalib was miserable and lonely. His friends were scattered, and he spent his time writing letters to them. These letters are of great literary and historical value.

But even in the midst of troubles, Ghalib never lost his sense of humour which was his shield against misfortunes. At one time, he was convinced that he would die in the Hijri year 1227, corresponding to 1860-61, but when he did not die, he pointed out that there had been an outbreak of cholera in Delhi and added, "My friend, I was not mistaken but I thought it beneath me to die in a general epidemic. Really it would have been an action unworthy of me. Once this trouble is over, we will see about it". Ghalib could write this when he was down in the dumps and his only hope lay in death. And when a friend congratulated him on this escape and sent an adulatory couplet, he said "For God's sake, compose no more verses in my name or I shall not shrink from claiming godhood for myself."

One of the highlights of Ghalib's letters of this time is the graphic pictures they paint of this choleric epidemic, a suffering to which the events of 1857 were only a prelude. Another aspect of these letters is the light they throw on his own condition and his attitude towards friends. It is noteworthy that when he was himself neck deep in trouble, he could go to any length to encourage and sustain his friends. A friend was depressed because a courtesan he loved very dearly had died. Ghalib wrote to him. "Friend, we Mughal lads, are death of those for whom we ourselves would die." He then refers to his own similar tragedy some forty year ago and reminds him of the transient nature of things of the world . He says, "you cannot mourn another man's death unless you live yourself. So, excessive grief is unmanly and one should go on with the business of life."

Ghalib was a very affectionate person. His friends were indeed very close to his heart. When Tufta wrote that he was afraid that Ghalib was displeased with him for something, Ghalib replied, "I pride myself that I have one friend in Hindustan who loves me, his name is Har Gopal and his pen name is Tufta." Besides letter writing, what occupied him in those days was correcting and polishing the verse of his friends. When Tufta wrote to him that he was afraid, he was sending him too many verses, Ghalib replied, 'God is my witness that you are a son to me. Hence the products of your inspiration are my spiritual grandchildren.' He would also help his pupils and friends to compose odes to various prospective patrons. But if he was kind, he could be very firm too. And he had a very independent approach to poetry and criticism, wherein he did not care much even for the greatest Persian authorities. If he showered affection on Tufta, he could snub him too. Once when Tufta complained of Ghalib's delay in returning to him his corrected verses, Ghalib reminded him that he was near his death and Tufta must not be unfair to him. In fact he gave him quite a piece of his mind.

While he helped his friends to write poems of praise to the patrons, he had nothing much to offer them from his own experience in this direction. In one rather, sorely humorous passage he says that his odes seem to have contrary effect:

"No one whom I praise survives it. One ode apiece was enough to dispatch Nasir and Amjad Ali Shah (king of Avadh), Wajid Ali Shah stood to three, and then collapsed. A man to whom I addressed ten or twenty odes ended upon the other side of oblivion."

In the last years of his life, his health started sharply deteriorating. He had started going deaf many years earlier, and was suffering from persistent boils and other maladies which he ascribed to overheating of blood. In 1863 he fell ill again, and this time it was a painful and a long illness, which left him depressed and embittered. The conduct of his friends at this time distressed him further. He told them that he was ill and should be forgiven if he could not reply to their letters or correct and send back their verses sooner. But most often they refused to listen. And then his memory began to fail him, and he would lose the ghazals that his friends sent him. Although there was an occasional improvement in his health, he never really recovered. But his friends continued to pester him. He wrote to one of them that his hands were trembling and his eyesight had gone much worse, adding that his senses were not with him. Even then he tried to answer the letters that his friends sent to him out of love.

In the month of February 1869, he was in his death-bed. According to Hali, a 'few days before his death he became unconscious for hours, recovering his senses only for a short interval before he lapsed again.' Hali says that he had gone to see him only a day before his death. He was dictating a reply to a letter from a friend from Lahore, who had enquired about his health. Ghalib replied "Why ask me how I am, wait for a day or two more and then ask my neighbours."

Ghalib carried with him a sense of injured merit, and died with the feeling that his age had not given him his due, had not recognised his full worth. He looked to posterity for the appreciation he deserved. He was confident that he would get it:

Today nobody is buying the wine of my poetry so that it may grow old to make the senses red in many a drinker yet to come. My star was shining highest in the sky before my birth, my poetry is going to win the world's acclaim after I am dead.

And he was right. Great poets are, indeed, prophets.

—**Kuldip Salil**

Contents

Ghazals

ग़ज़लें

हज़ारों ख़्वाहिशें ऐसी, कि हर ख़्वाहिश पे दम निकले
बहुत निकले मेरे अरमान, लेकिन फिर भी कम निकले

निकलना ख़ुल्द[1] से आदम का सुनते आए थे, लेकिन
बहुत बेआबरू हो कर तिरे कूचे से हम निकले

हुई जिनसे तवक़्क़ो, ख़स्तगी[2] की दाद पाने की
वो हम से भी ज़ियादा ख़स्त-ए-तेग़ो-सितम[3] निकले

मुहब्बत में नहीं है फ़र्क़, जीने और मरने का
उसी को देख कर जीते हैं, जिस काफ़िर पे दम निकले

ख़ुदा के वास्ते पर्दा न काबे का उठा वाइज़
कहीं ऐसा न हो यां भी वही काफ़िर सनम निकले

कहाँ मैख़ाने का दरवाज़ा, 'ग़ालिब', और कहाँ वाइज़
पर इतना जानते हैं, कल वो जाता था, कि हम निकले

Hazaron Khwahishen Aisi ki her khwahish pe dum nikle
Bahut nikle mere armaan, lekin phir bhi kum nikle

Nikalna khuld se aadam ka sunte aaye the, lekin
bahut beaabru ho kar tirey kuche se hum nikle

Hui jinse tawaqqo, khastagi ki daad pane ki
woh humse bhi jiyada khast-e-tege-sitam nikle

Muhabbat mein nahin hai farq, jine aur marne ka
usi ko dekh kar jite hain, jis kafir pe dum nikle

Khuda ke vaste parda ne kaabe ka utha waiz
kahin aisa na ho yaan bhi vahi kafir sanam nikle

Kahan maikhane ka darwaga, 'Ghalib' aur kahan waiz
par itna jante hain, kal woh jata tha, ki hum nikle

---

1. स्वर्ग 2. पागलपन 3. अत्याचार की तलवार के घायल

30

Thousands of desires, life-consuming and tough
I had them fulfilled in plenty, but not enough

Expulsion of man from paradise we had known
But how disgracefully from your street we've been
thrown

The people, who we thought, would commiserate
with us in distress
Themselves turned to be more oppressed, not less

In love, there is no difference between life and death
We die for the same infidel who is our life's breath

For heaven's sake, do not open the door of Kaba,
lest there too I should see
The same infidel, looking at me bewitchingly

Is there any relation between the door of the tavern
and the preacher, please say
But believe me, as I was coming out, he was going in
yesterday

कभी नेकी भी उसके जी में गर आ जाए है मुझसे
जफ़ायें करके अपनी याद शर्मा जाए है मुझसे

ख़ुदाया, जज़्ब-ए-दिल की मगर तासीर उल्टी है
कि जितना खेंचता हूँ उतना खिंचता जाये है मुझसे

उधर वो बदगुमानी है, इधर यह नातवानी[1] है
न पूछा जाये है उससे, न बोला जाये है मुझसे

सँभलने दे मुझे, ऐ नाउमीदी, क्या क़यामत है
कि दामाने-ख्याले-यार, छूटा जाये है मुझसे

हुए हैं पाँव ही पहले नबर्दे-इश्क़[2] में ज़ख़्मी
न भागा जाए है मुझसे, न ठहरा जाए है मुझसे

क़यामत है, कि होवे मुद्दई का हमसफ़र, 'ग़ालिब'
वो काफ़िर, जो ख़ुदा को भी न सौंपा जाए है मुझसे

Kabhi neki bhi uskey ji mein gar aa jaye hai mujhse
Zafayein karke apni yaad sharma jaye hai mujhse

Khudaya, zazab-e-dil ki magar taasir ulti hai
ki jitna khenchta hun utna khinchta jaye hai mujhse

Udhar woh badgumani hai, idhar yeh naatwani hai
ne puchha jaye hai ussey, na bola jaye hai mujhse

Sambhalne de mujhe, ai naummidi, kya qayamat hai
ki damaney-khayale-yaar, chhuta jaye hai mujhse

Huye hain paon hi pahale nabarde-ishaq mein zakhami
ne bhaga jaye hai mujhse, na thehra jaye hai mujhse

Qayamat hai, ki howe muddai ka humsafar, 'Ghalib'
Woh Kafir, jo khuda ko bhi na saunpa jaye hai mujhse

---

1. निर्बलता 2. प्रेम का संघर्ष

If ever she thinks of being to me a little kind
She's abashed as her cruelties cross her mind

The desire of my heart, O God has but a contrary
effect
More she goes away from me, as more I try to attract

There, it is such arrogance, such feebleness here
That neither can I speak, nor will she enquire my
welfare

Let me hold myself together, O despair
O damn it, I cannot hold on to the thought of a
friend fair

Because of wandering in love, my feet are just undone
I neither can stay put nor can I run

O misery, that she should with my rival be
She, whom, O Ghalib, even with God I cannot see

वो फ़िराक़ और वो विसाल' कहाँ
वो शबो-रोज़ो-माहो-साल² कहाँ

फ़ुर्सते - कारोबारे - शौक़³ किसे
ज़ौक़े - नज़्ज़ार - ए - जमाल⁴ कहाँ

थी वो इक शख़्स के तसव्वुर से
अब वो रानाइ-ए-ख़यालᵉ कहाँ

ऐसा आसां नहीं, लहू रोना
दिल में ताक़त, जिगर में हाल कहाँ

हमसे छूटा क़िमारख़ान-ए-इश्क़⁶
वां जो जावें, गिरह में माल कहाँ

फ़िक्रे-दुनिया में सर खपाता हूँ
मैं कहाँ और यह वबाल कहाँ

मुज़महिल⁷ हो गए क़ुवा⁸ 'ग़ालिब'
वो अनासिर⁹ में एतिदाल¹⁰ कहाँ

Woh firaq aur woh visaal kahan
woh shabo-rozo-maho-saal kahan

Phursate - karobare - shauq kise
zokey - nazzar - e- jamal kahan

Thi woh ik shaksh ke tasavoor se
ab woh ranai-e-khayal kahan

Aisa aasan nahin, lahoo rona
dil mein taquat, jigar mein haal kahan

Humse chhuta qimarkhan-e-ishq
wan jo jawen, girah mein maal kahan

Phikre duniya mein sir khapata hun
Main kahan aur yeh bawaal kahan

Muzmahil ho gaye quwa 'Ghalib'
woh anasir mein etidaal kahan

---

1. मिलन 2. रात दिन मास वर्ष 3. सांसारिक व्यापार के लिए अवकाश 4. सौन्दर्य का दृश्य
देखने की अभिरुचि 5. कल्पना का शृंगार 6. प्रेम का जुआघर 7. शिथिल 8. शक्तियाँ
9. तत्त्व 10. सन्तुलन।

No more that union, that separation no more
No more the day and night and the year and month
of yore

Where is the time now for love's labour
Who longs to feed on beauty, any longer

All because of our imagining of her, it had been
No more is now that lustre seen

Weeping blood is no child's play
Where is the strength in the heart, where that firm
resolve, today

The gaming house of love—No more do I go there
For I am left with nothing now to wager

Worrying about the world, I wraek my brain
O for a man like me, an endeavour how vain!

Our youthful strength Ghalib, is a thing of the past
And the elements have their harmony lost

बाज़ीच-ए-अत्फ़ाल' है दुनिया मेरे आगे
होता है शबो रोज़ तमाशा, मेरे आगे

इक खेल है औरंगे-सुलेमां², मेरे नज़दीक
इक बात है, ऐजाज़े-मसीहा³, मेरे आगे

होता है निहां गर्द में सहरा, मेरे होते
घिसता है जबीं⁴ खाक प दरिया मेरे आगे

मत पूछ, कि क्या हाल है मेरा, तेरे पीछे
तू देख, कि क्या रंग है तेरा, मेरे आगे

ईमां मुझे रोके है, तो खेंचे है मुझे कुफ़्र
काबा मेरे पीछे है, कलीसा⁵ मेरे आगे

ख़ुश होते हैं पर वस्ल में यूँ मर नहीं जाते
आई शबे-हिजरां⁶ की तमन्ना मेरे आगे

गो हाथ को जुम्बिश नहीं, आँखों में तो दम है
रहने दो अभी सागर-ओ-मीना मिरे आगे

हम-पेश-ओ-हम-मशरब-ओ-हमराज़ है मेरा
'ग़ालिब' को बुरा क्यों, कहो अच्छा, मेरे आगे।

Bajich-e-atfal hai duniya mere aagey
hota hai shabo roz tamasha mere aagey

Ik khel hai Aurange-sulema, mere nazdik
Ik baat hai, ejaze-masiha, mere aagey

Hota hai nihan gurd mein sehara, mere hote
ghista hai jabin khaaq pe dariya mere aagey

Mat puchh, ki kya haal hai mera, tere pichhey
Tu dekh, ki kya rang hai tera, mere aagey

Imaan mujhe roke hai, to khenchey hai mujhe kufra
kaba mere pichhe hai, kalisau mere aagey

Khush hote hain per vasal mein yun mar nahin jatey
Aai shabe-hijra ki tamanna mere aagey

Go hath ko jumbish nahin, aankhon mein to dum hai
rahane do abhi sagar-o-meena mirey aagey

Hum-pesh-o-hum-mashrub-o-hum-raaz hai mera
'Ghablib' ko bura kyon, kaho achha, mere aagey

---

1. बच्चों का खेल 2. सुलेमान का राजसिंहासन 3. ईसा का चमत्कार (ईसा की फूँक से मुर्दे जी
उठते थे) 4. माथा 5. गिरजाघर 6. विरह यामिनी।

This world for me is but a childrens' playground
Where day and night a funny something is happening
around

Solomon's throne for me is only a plaything
And Christ's miracle an ordinary something

Under the dust raised by me, I see a desert hidden
around
And the river before me rubs its forehead on the
ground

Ask not how I fare in your absence
But see how you look in my presence

Truth pulls at me as falsehood attractive I find
The cathedral is in my front, the Kaba behind

Be happy on meeting, but go not overboard prithee
I am haunted by the joys of separation already

My hands are lifeless though, my eyes are still bright
Remove not the cup and the bottle yet from my sight

Ghalib is a colleague, co-professional and a comrade
Call him good before me, rather than degrade

दिल ही तो है न संगो-ख़िश्त', दर्द से भर न आए क्यों
रोयेंगे हम हज़ार बार, कोई हमें सताए क्यों

दैर नहीं, हरम नहीं, दर नहीं, आस्तां नहीं
बैठे हैं रहगुज़र पे हम, कोई हमें उठाए क्यों

जब वो जमाले-दिल-फ़रोज़' सूरते-मेहरे-नीमरोज़'
आप ही हो नज़ारा सोज़, पर्दे में मुँह छिपाये क्यों

क़ैदे-हयातो-बन्दे-ग़म', अस्ल में दोनों एक हैं
मौत से पहले आदमी ग़म से नजात पाए क्यों

वां वो गुरूरे-इज़्ज़ो-नाज़' यां यह हिजाबे-पासे-वज़अ'
राह में हम मिलें कहाँ, बज़्म में वो बुलाए क्यों

हाँ वो नहीं ख़ुदा परस्त, जाओ वो बेवफ़ा सही
जिसको हो दीनो-दिल अज़ीज़, उसकी गली में जाए क्यों

'ग़ालिबे'-ख़स्ता' के बिग़ैर कौन से काम बंद हैं
रोइए ज़ार-ज़ार' क्या कीजिए हाय हाय क्यों

Dil hi to hai na sango-khisht, dard se bhar na aaye kyon
royenge hum hazar baar, koi hamein sataye kyon

Dair nahin, harum nahin, dar nahin, aastan nahin
Baithe hain rahguzar pe hum, koi hamain uthaye kyon

Jab woh jamale-dil-raroz suratey-mehare-neemroz
aap hi ho nazara soaj, pardey mein muhn chhipaye kyon

Qaide-hayato-bande-ghum, asal mein dono ek hain
maut se pahale aadmi gum se najat paye kyon

Wan woh gururey-izzo-naaz yaan yeha hijabe-paase-vaza
Raah mein hum miley kahan, bazm mein woh bulaey kyon

Haan woh nahin khuda parast, jao woh bewafa sahi
jisko ho dino-dil aziz, uski gali mein jaye kyon

'Ghalibe'-khasta ke begair kaun se kaam band hain
roiye zaar-zaar kya kijiye haye-haye kyon

---

1. ईंट पत्थर 2. मन को प्रकाशित करने वाला रूप 3. दोपहर के सूर्य की भाँति 4. जीवन-कारा
और दुख बंधन 5. अपनी शान का गर्व 6. अपनी व्यवहार प्रणाली कों न बदलने का संकोच
7. दुर्दशाग्रस्त ग़ालिब 8. फूट-फूट कर

It is heart after all, not brick and stone, why won't
it well up with pain,
Why should anybody harass us, we shall a
thousand times cry

No home, no hearth for us, no temple, no mosque
Why should anybody remove us from the thorough
fare, can we ask

Her beauty illumines all, a full waxing moon in grace
Loveliness incarnate indeed, why should she hide
her face

Life's incarceration and bondage to suffering are the
same thing indeed
Untill our death how can we from suffering be relieved

She is puffed up with status high, and we have to
keep our self-respect right
How can we meet half way, why would she to his
gathering invite

Alright, she is not kindhearted, nor faithful she, so
Why should anybody who loves, his faith and
life, go to her street

What business of life, without Ghalib the
miserable, has shut its door
Why should anybody cry his heart out if he's no
more

इब्ने-मरियम¹ हुआ करे कोई
मेरे दुख की दवा करे कोई

बात पर वां ज़ुबान कटती है
वो कहें और सुना करे कोई

बक रहा हूँ जुनूं में क्या क्या कुछ
कुछ न समझे, ख़ुदा करे कोई

रोक लो, गर ग़लत चले कोई
बख़्श दो, गर ख़ता करे कोई

कौन है, जो नहीं है हाजतमंद²
किसकी हाजत रवा करे कोई

क्या किया ख़िज़्र³ ने सिकंदर से
अब किसे रहनुमा करे कोई

जब तवक़्क़ो⁴ ही उठ गई 'ग़ालिब'
क्यों किसी का गिला करे कोई

Ibne-mariam hua karey koi
mere dukh ki dawa karey koi

Baat per waan zuban katati hai
woh kahen aur suna karey koi

Bak raha hun junun mein kya kya kuchh
kuchh na samjhe, khuda karey koi

Rok lo, gar galat chaley koi
baksh do, gar khata karey koi

Kaun hai, jo nahin hai hajatmand
kiski haajat rawa karey koi

Kya kiya khizra ne Sikandar se
ab kisey rehnuma karey koi

Jab tawaqqo hi utha gai 'Ghalib'
kyon kisi ka gila karey koi

1. मरियम का पुत्र ईसा 2. ज़रूरतमंद 3. एक पैगम्बर जो भूले-भटकों को राह दिखाते हैं
4. आशा

What if somebody son of Mary be
Unless he cures me of my misery

Utter a word there, and your tongue is gone
You cannot but listen, when she is on

I do not know what I gibber in this fit
May God, nobody know it

Stop him if a wrong road he takes
Forgive him if somebody makes a mistake

Is there anyone who is not needy
Then the demand of how many can one possibly
meet

What good to Sikander could Khizra, the Prophet
do
Who could be our guide then, who?

O Ghalib, when expectation itself doesn't remain
Why should one against anybody complain

सब कहाँ-कुछ लाल-ओ-गुल' में नुमायां' हो गई
ख़ाक में क्या सूरतें होंगीं, कि पिन्हा हो गई

जू-ए-खूं' आँखों से बहने दो, कि है शामे-फ़िराक़
मैं यह समझूँगा, कि शम्एं दो फ़रोज़ां' हो गई

इन परीज़ादों से लेंगे ख़ुल्द में हम इन्तिक़ाम
क़ुदरते-हक़ से, यही हूरें अगर वां हो गई

नींद उसकी है, दिमाग़ उसका है, रातें उसकी हैं
तेरी ज़ुल्फ़ें, जिसके बाज़ू पर परीशां हो गई

वां गया भी मैं, तो उनकी गालियों का क्या जवाब
याद थी जितनी दुआएँ, सर्फ़े-दरबां हो गई।

रंज से ख़ूगर' हुआ इंसां, तो मिट जाता है रंज
मुश्किलें मुझ पर पड़ीं इतनी कि आसां हो गई।

यूं ही गर रोता रहा 'ग़ालिब', तो ऐ अहले-जहाँ'
देखना इन बस्तियों को तुम, कि वीराँ हो गई।

Sab kahan-kuchh laal-o-gul mein numayan ho gai
khaak mein kya suratein hongi, ki pinha ho gai

Ju-e-khun aankhon se behane do, ki hai shamey-firaq
main yeha samjhunga, ki shamae do pharozan ho gai

In parizadon se lengey khuld mein hum intikaam
qudratey-huq se, yahi hurein agar waan ho gai

Neend uski hai, dimaag uska hai, ratein uski hain
teri zulphen, jiskey bazu par parishan ho gai

Waan gaya bhi main, to unki galiyon ka kya jawab
yaad thi jitnee duaen, surphey-darban ho gai

ranj se khugar hua insaan, to mit jata hai ranj
mushkilen mujh par parin itnee ki asaan ho gai

Yun hi gar rota raha 'Ghalib', to ai ahley-jahan
dekhna in bastiyon ko tum, ki veeran ho gai

---

1. लाले तथा गुलाब के फूल 2. प्रकट 3. रक्त की नदी 4. प्रज्ज्वलित 5. परी; अप्सरा
6. अभ्यस्त 7. ऐ दुनिया वालो

What shapes and forms must lie buried in dust
Not all, but only a few in the form of flowers
burst

If a stream of blood flows from my eyes this evening
of separation, it's alright
I'll take it that two bright candles have come to light

If by some miracle they can do that place make
In heaven, surely we'll on the beauties our revenge
take

The nights are really his, his is the sleep, he alone
can proud be
On whose arm you allow your tresses to flow free

What possibly, will now my response to her abuses be
For, I have expended all the prayers I knew to the
doorkeeper already

Once you get used to sorrow, sorrow it ceases to be
So many hardships befell me that they became easy

If Ghalib keeps weeping like this, O people of the
world
You will soon see these towns into wilderness
hurled

क़दो-गेसू[1] में क़ैसो-कोहकन[2] की आज़माइश है
जहाँ हम हैं वहाँ दारो-रसन[3] की आज़माइश है

करेंगे कोहकन के हौसले का इम्तिहां आख़िर
हनोज़ उस ख़स्ता के नीरू-ए-तन[4] की आज़माइश है

वो आया बज़्म में, देखो न कहियो फिर कि ग़ाफ़िल थे
शिकेबो-सब्रे-अहले-अंजुमन[5] की आज़माइश है

रहे-दिल ही में तीर अच्छा, जिगर के पार हो बेहतर
ग़रज़ शिस्ते-बुते-नावक फ़िगन[6] की आज़माइश है

पड़ा रह ऐ दिले - वाबस्ता बेताबी से क्या हासिल
मगर फिर ताबे-ज़ुल्फ़े-पुरशिकन[7] की आज़माइश है

Qado-gesu mein qaiso-kohkan ki aajmaish hai
jahan hum hain wahan daaro-rasan ki aajmaish hai

Karengey kohkan ke hausaley ka imtihaan aakhir
hanoz us khasta ke neeru-e-tan ki aajmaish hai

Woh aaya bazm mein, dekho na kahiyo phir ki ghafil the
shikebo-sabrey-ahley-anjuman ki aajmaish hai

Rahe-dil hi mein teer achha, jigar ke paar ho behtar
garaz shishtey-bute-navak phigan ki aajmaish hai

Para raha ai diley -wabasta betabi se kya hasil
magar phir tabey-zulphe-purshikan ki aajmaish hai

---

1. आकार और पलकें 2. मजनूं और फरहाद 3. सूली और फांसी का फंदा 4. शारीरिक शक्ति
5. महफिल वालों का धैर्य और संतोष 6. तीर चलाने वाले माशूक का निशाना 7. घुँघराले
बालों की शक्ति

44

By the stature and tresses of their beloveds, Farhad
                    and Qais were tested at their best
In our case it is the gallows and the hangman's noose
                    that are on test

On test ultimately is Farhad's courage and what he can
On test now is the physical strength of the frail man

He has come to the assembly, see, you cannot
                    afford to show indifference
On test, in fact, now is the assembly's capacity and
                    patience

Good, if the arrow remains lodged in the heart,
                    better if it pierces it
On test now is the arrow-wielding beloved's ability to hit

Hold on, my over-eager heart, and your impatience
                    eschew
And be rather warned of what the curly hair can do.

हुस्ने-मह', गरचे बहंगामे-कमाल² अच्छा है
उससे मेरा महे-ख़ुर्शीद जमाल अच्छा है

उनके देखे से, जो आ जाती है, मुँह पर रौनक़
वो समझते हैं कि बीमार का हाल अच्छा है

देखिए, पाते हैं उश्शाक़, बुतों से क्या फ़ैज़
इक बिरहमन ने कहा है, कि यह साल अच्छा है

क़तरा दरिया में जो मिल जाए, तो दरिया हो जाए
काम अच्छा है वो, जिसका कि मआल³ अच्छा है

हमको मालूम है, जन्नत की हक़ीक़त⁴ लेकिन
दिल के.ख़ुश रखने को, 'ग़ालिब', यह ख्याल अच्छा है।

Husney-meh, garche bahungame kamal achha hai
usse mera mahe-khursheed jamal achha hai

Unke dekhey se, jo aa jaati hai, munha par raunaq
woh samajhte hain ki bimaar ka haal achha hai

Dekhiye patein hain ushshaaq, buton se kya faiz
ik birahaman ne kaha hai, ki yeh saal achha hai

Qatra dariya mein jo mil jaye, to dariya to jaye
kaam achha hai woh, jiska ki meaal achha hai

Humko maloom hai, jannat ki haqiqat lekin
dil ke khush rakhne ko, 'Ghalib', yeh khayal achha hai

---

1. चन्द्रमा का सौन्दर्य 2. पूर्ण चन्द्र होने का समय 3. अन्त; परिणाम 4. स्वर्ग की वास्तविकता

46

Beauty of the full waxing moon though complete
It cannot with the moonlike face of my beloved
compete

If on her arrival, my face puts on a glow
She thinks that the patient does improvement
show

Let us see what bounty from the beauties they procure
A Brahmin says that the lovers have a good year in store

It becomes the river itself, the drop that doth in the
river gel
Only what ends well, is well

Though we know full well the truth about heaven
As a surmise, Ghalib, it is a pleasing one

दरखुरे-कहरो-ग़ज़ब', जब कोई हम सा न हुआ
फिर ग़लत क्या है कि हम सा कोई पैदा न हुआ

बन्दगी में भी, वो आज़ाद-ओ-खुदबीं² हैं कि हम
उल्टे फिर आएँ, दरे-काबा अगर वा न हुआ

सीने का दाग़ है, वो नाला, कि लब तक न गया
ख़ाक़ का रिज़्क़ है वो क़तरा, कि दरिया न हुआ

क़तरे में दजला दिखाई न दे, और जुज़्व में कुल
खेल लड़कों का हुआ, दीद-ए-बीना³ न हुआ

थी ख़बर गर्म, कि 'ग़ालिब' के उड़ेंगे पुर्ज़े
देखने हम भी गए थे, पे तमाशा न हुआ

Darkhure-kaharo-ghazab, jub koi hum sa na hua
phir galat kya hai ki hum sa koi paida na hua

Bandagi mein bhi, woh azad-o-khudbin hain ki hum
ulte phir aayen, darey-kaba agar waa na hua

Seeney ka daag hai, woh nala, ki lub tak na gaya
khaaq ki rizak hai woh qatra, ki dariya na hua

Qatrey mein dajla dikhai na de, aur zuzav mein kul
khel larkon ka hua, deed-e-beena na hua

Thi khabar garm, ki 'Ghalib' ke urengey purzey
dekhane hum bhi gaye the, pe tamasha na hua

---

1. प्रकोप तथा आपत्ति के योग्य 2. मनमौजी और अभिमानी 3. द्रष्टा की आँख

48

None but I could bear the barbs and tortures she inflicted
So, obviously nobody like me has existed

Such is my sense of self-respect that even though I went to pray
If the doors of Kaba were not open, I came away

The cry that did not find expression became a festering wound
It is swallowed by the sand, the drop that has not a river found

If it doesn't see an ocean in a drop, or in a speck, the sky
It's a childish ken, not a seeing eye

Ghalib will be torn to pieces, the news was hot
We too went to witness the fun, but it was not

फिर मुझे दीद-ए-तर याद आया
दिल, जिगर तश्न-ए-फरियाद आया

दम लिया था न क़यामत ने हनोज़[1]
फिर तिरा वक़्ते-सफ़र याद आया।

ज़िन्दगी यों भी गुज़र ही जाती
क्यों तेरा राहगुज़र याद आया

फिर तेरे कूचे को जाता है ख़याल
दिले-गुमगश्ता[2] मगर याद आया

कोई वीरानी सी वीरानी है
दश्त को देख के घर याद आया

मैंने मजनूं प लड़कपन में, 'असद'
संग उठाया था, कि सर याद आया

Phir mujhe deed-e-tar yaad aaya
dil, jigar tashan-e-phariyad aaya

Dum liya tha na qayamat ne hanoz
phir tira waqte-safar yaad aaya

Zindagi yon bhi guzar hi jaati
kyon tera raahguzar yaad aaya

Phir terey kuchey ko jaata hai khyal
diley-gumgashta magar yaad aaya

Koi veerani si veerani hai
dasht ko dekh ke ghar yaad aaya

Maine majnu pe ladakpan mein, 'Asad'
sang uthaya tha, ki sir yaad aaya

---

1. अभी 2. खोया हुआ दिल

50

Again I remember my moist eye
Again I wish to complain and cry

The doom's day was hardly over
When once again the time of your departure, I
　　　　　　　　　　　　　　remember

Life would have passed in any case, then why
Did I remember the road you went by

Again to her street doth the mind wander
But in the meantime, the heart lost there, I remember

What desolation doth, O God, here fall
As I see the forest, my home I recall

For Majnu's head in my boyhood, 'Asad', as I lifted a
　　　　　　　　　　　　　　　　stone
I instantly remembered my own

नुक़्ताचीं¹ है ग़मे-दिल उसको सुनाये न बने
क्या बने बात, जहाँ बात बनाए न बने

मैं बुलाता तो हूँ उसको, मगर ऐ जज़्ब-ए-दिल²
उस पे बन जाए कुछ ऐसी, कि बिन आए न बने

ग़ैर फिरता है, लिये यों तिरे ख़त को, कि अगर
कोई पूछे कि यह क्या है, तो छुपाये न बने

इस नज़ाकत का बुरा हो, वो भले हैं तो क्या
हाथ आएँ, तो उन्हें हाथ लगाए न बने

बोझ वो सर से गिरा है, कि उठाये न उठे
काम वो आन पड़ा है, कि बनाये न बने

इश्क़ पर ज़ोर नहीं, है ये वो आतिश, 'ग़ालिब'
कि लगाये न लगे और बुझाये न बने

Nuktachin hai gamey-dil usko sunaye na bane
kya bane baat, jahan baat banaye na bane

Main bulata to hun usko, magar ae zazab-e-dil
us pe ban jaye kuchh aisi, ki bin aaye ne bane

Gair phirta hai, liye yon tirey khat ko, ki agar
koi puchhey ki yeh kya hai, to chhupaye na bane

Is nazakat ka bura ho, woh bhaley hain to kya
hath aayen, to unhe hath lagaye na bane

Bojh woh sir se gira hai, ki uthay na uthey
kaam woh aan para hai, ki banaye na bane

Ishq par zor nahin hai ye woh aatish 'Ghalib'
ki lagaye na lagey aur bujhaye na bane

---

1. हर बात में दोष निकालने वाला माशूक 2. मनोभाव

She is so dismissive, O wretched heart, that she
hears no plea
How can you solve a problem, for which just no
solution be

I invite her, of course, but O heart, so fashion it
That she cannot but pay me a visit

My rival goes about carrying your letter to my spite
And if somebody asks him what it is, he is overcome
with delight

Damned be this delicacy, what use is nobleness such
That even when she is with me, I cannot touch

I just cannot lift the luggage fallen from my head
O, beyond me is the job that lies ahead

It is a fire which neither can be lighted, nor put out
Love, O Ghalib accepts no prompting from without

किसी को देके दिल कोई नवा संजे-फुगां क्यों हो
न हो जब दिल ही सीने में, तो फिर मुँह में जुबां क्यों हो

वो अपनी खू न छोड़ेंगे, हम अपनी वज़्अ क्यों बदलें
सुबुक सर¹ बन के क्या पूछें कि हमसे सरगिरां² क्यों हो

किया ग़मख़्वार ने रुस्वा, लगे आग इस मुहब्बत को
न लावे ताब जो ग़म की, वो मेरा राज़दां क्यों हो

वफ़ा कैसी, कहाँ का इश्क़, जब सर फोड़ना ठहरा
तो फिर, ऐ संग दिल, तेरा ही संगे-आस्तां क्यों हो

क़फ़स³ में मुझसे रूदादे-चमन⁴ कहते, न डर, हमदम
गिरी है जिस पे कल बिजली, वो मेरा आशियां क्यों हो

यह फ़ितना, आदमी की ख़ाना वीरानी को क्या कम है
हुए तुम दोस्त जिसके, दुश्मन उसका आस्मां क्यों हो

यही है आज़माना, तो सताना किसको कहते हैं
अदू⁵ के हो लिए जब तुम, तो मेरा इम्तिहां क्यों हो

निकाला चाहता है काम क्या तानों से तू, 'ग़ालिब'
तेरे बेमेहर⁶ कहने से, वो तुझ पर मेहरबां क्यों हो

Kisi ko deke dil koi nawa sanje-phugan kyon ho
na ho jab dil hi seeney mein, to phir munha mein zuban kyon ho

Woh apni khu na chhorengey, hum apni waza kyon badlein
subuk sir ban ke kya puchhein ki humse sirgiran kyon ho

Kiya ghumkhwar ne ruswa, lagey aag is muhabbat ko
na laawe taab jo ghm ki, woh mera raazdan kyon ho

Wafa kaisi, kahan ka ishq, jub sir phorna thera
to phir, ai sang dil, tera hi sange-aastan kyon ho

Qafas mein mujhse rudadey-chaman kehte, na dar, humdum
giri hai jis pe kal bijali, woh mera aashiyan kyon ho

Yeh fitna, aadmi ki khana veerani ko kya kam hai
huye tum dost jiskey, dushman uska aasman kyon ho

Yahi hai aazmana, to satana kisko kehte hain
adu ke ho liye jab tum, to mera imtihaan kyon ho

Nikala chahata hai kaam kya tanon se tu, 'Ghalib'
tere bemehar kehne se, woh tujh pr meharban kyon ho

---

1. अपमानित 2. अप्रसन्न 3. पिंजरा 4. उद्यान का हाल 5. शत्रु 6 प्रेमविहीन

After losing the heart to somebody, why should
one grumble and sigh
When there is no heart in the breast, why should
the tongue in the mouth lie

She will not change his attitude, then why should
my ways be changed
Why humiliate myself, and ask her why he is estranged

Damned be this love, my friend annoyed I see
If he cannot bear with my grief, how can he a friend
be

What fealty, what love, if I have to break my head
against a stone
And then, O stone-hearted one, why should it be
your door-step alone

Fear not, and the garden's tale to me in the prison
freely say
Why should it belong to me, the nest hit by the
lightning yesterday

To what misery won't this misfortune lead
With you as a friend, why should one an enemy need

If this is testing, then what's torturing?
If you are for my foe, then why me are you testing

Ghalib, what purpose would it serve, that you taunt
her, as you do
Do you think, if you call her unkind, she will be kind
to you.

आह को चाहिए इक उम्र, असर होने तक
कौन जीता है तिरी जुल्फ़ के सर होने तक

दामे-हर मौज में है, हलक़-ए-सदकामे-निहंग[1]
देखें क्या गुज़रे है, क़तरे प गुहर होने तक

आशिक़ी सब्र तलब और तमन्ना बेताब
दिल का क्या रंग करूँ, ख़ूने-जिगर होने तक

हमने माना, कि तग़ाफुल[2] न करोगे, लेकिन
ख़ाक हो जाएँगे हम, तुमको ख़बर होने तक

परतवे-ख़ुर से है शबनम को, फ़ना की तालीम
मैं भी हूँ, एक इनायत की नज़र होने तक

यक नज़र बेश नहीं, फुर्सते-हस्ती ग़ाफ़िल
गर्मि-ए-बज़्म[3] है, इक रक़्से-शरर[4] होने तक

ग़मे-हस्ती का, 'असद' किससे हो जुज़ मर्ग[5] इलाज
शम्अ हर रंग में जलती है सहर होने तक

Aah ko chahiye ik umra, asar hone tak
kaun jita hai tiri zulf ke sir hone tak

Daame-har mauj mein hai, halaq-e-sadkame-nihung
dekhen kya guzrey hai, katre pe guhar hone tak

Aashiqi subra talab aur tamanna betaab
dil ka kya rung karoon, khune-jigar hone tak

Humne mana, ki taghaphul na karoge, lekin
khaak ho jayenge hum, tumko khabar hone tak

Partave-khur se hai shabnam ko, phana ki taleem
main bhi hun, ek inayat ki nazar hone tak

Yak nazar besh nahin, phursate-hasti gaphil
garmi-e-bazm hai, ik rakse-sharar hone tak

Game-hasti ka, 'Asad' kis se ho juz murg ilaj
shamae har rung mein jalti hai sehar hone tak

---

1. मगरमच्छ के सैकड़ों जबड़े 2. उपेक्षा 3. महफिल की गर्मी 4. चिंगारी का नृत्य 5. मृत्यु के अतिरिक्त

It needs a whole age for a sigh to reach somewhere
Who lives long enough to conquer the heart of his
beloved fair

Every wave has in it a thousand hazards entwined
Let us see, how fares the drop till a pearl we can find

Desire is impatient and love much patience needs
O what do I do of the heart while the liver bleeds

You'll not be indifferent, I entirely trust
But by the time you come to know, I shall be reduced
to dust

As the sun shoots its ray, a dew drop goes away
I too am around till a kindly glance comes my way

Life is not more than a moment's parole, O man
Its warmth can last not longer than a dancing flame can

Life's suffering has no end, 'Asad', except demise
The candle burns in any case, till the dawn arrives

मुद्दत हुई है यार को मेहमां किये हुए
जोशे-क़दह[1] से, बज़्म चराग़ां किये हुए

दिल फिर तवाफ़े-कू-ए मलामत[2] को जाये है
पिन्दार[3] का सनमकदा वीरां किये हुए

फिर शौक़ कर रहा है ख़रीददार की तलब
अर्ज़े-मता-ए-अक़्ल-ओ-दिल-ओ-जां[4] किए हुए

मांगे है फिर, किसी को लबे-बाम[5] पर, हवस
ज़ुल्फ़े-सियाह रुख़ पे परीशां किये हुए

इक नौबहारे-नाज़[6] को ताके है फिर, निगाह
चेहरा फ़रोग़े-मै से गुलिस्तां किये हुए

फिर, जी में है कि दर पे किसी के पड़े रहें
सर ज़ेरे-बारे-मिन्नते-दरबां किये हुए

जी ढूँढ़ता है फिर वही फ़ुर्सत, कि रात दिन
बैठे रहें तसव्वुरे-जानां किये हुए

Muddat hui hai yaar ko mehmaan kiye huye
joshe-qadah se, bazm charaghan kiye huye

Dil phir tawaphe-ku-e malamat ko jaye hai
pindaar ka sanamkada veeran kiye huye

Phir shauq kar raha hai khariddar ki talab
arze-mata-e-akal-o-dil-o-jaan kiye huye

Mangey hai phir, kisi ko labe-baam par, havas
Zulphe-siyaah rukh pe parishan kiye huye

Ik naubahare-naaz ko takey hai phir, nigaah
chehra pharoge-mai se gulistan kiye hue

Phir, ji mein hai ki dar pe kisi ke parey rahein
sir zerey-barey-minnate-darban kiye huye

Ji dhundhta hai phir wahi phursat, ke raat din
Baithein rahen tasavoore-janan kiye huye

---

1. मदिरा का उबाल 2. धिक्कार की गली की परिक्रमा 3. घमंड 4. बुद्धि, मन और प्राण की संपत्ति का समर्पण 5. छत पर 6. सौन्दर्याभिमान की नई बहार में डूबा हुआ आकार

It is ages now that we were by our friend visited
And had the house with cups of wine illuminated

To the winds, once again, all my ego throwing
I feel like to that street of my infamy going

For my heart, my soul and the mind
My love would fain a customer find

Her black tresses spread all around her face
My passion once again wants somebody on the
terrace

With her face all flush and blooming with wine
A fresh coquettish beauty is the wish of these eyes of
mine

My head, out of gratitude to the gatekeeper bowing
Once again, I feel like on her doorstep sprawling

To keep sitting, wrapped in thoughts of the beloved
sleek
Once again, those days and nights of leisure doth
the heart seek

दिले-नादां¹, तुझे हुआ क्या है
आख़िर इस दर्द की दवा क्या है

हम हैं मुश्ताक़² और वो बेज़ार³
या इलाही, यह माजरा⁴ क्या है

मैं भी मुँह में जुबान रखता हूँ
काश, पूछो कि मुद्आ क्या है

हमको उनसे, वफ़ा की है उम्मीद
जो नहीं जानते वफ़ा क्या है

हाँ भला कर, तिरा भला होगा
और दरवेश की सदा क्या है

जान तुम पर निसार करता हूँ
मैं नहीं जानता, दुआ क्या है

मैंने माना कि कुछ नहीं 'ग़ालिब'
मुफ़्त हाथ आये, तो बुरा क्या है

Diley-nadan, tujhe hua kya hai
aakhir is dard ki dawa kya hai

Hum hain mushtaq aur woh bezaar
ya ilahi, yeh majra kya hai

Main bhi munha mein zuban rakhta hoon
kash, puchho ki mudda kya hai

Humko unse, wafa ki hai ummid
jo nahin jante wafa kya hai

Haan bhala kar, tira bhala hoga
aur darvesh ki sada kya hai

Jaan tum par nisaar karta hoon
main nahin janta, dua kya hai

Maine mana ki kuchh nahin 'Ghalib'
muft hath aaye, to bura kya hai

---

1. बावरे मन 2. उत्सुक 3. असंतुष्ट 4. मामला

O my fond heart, what is it that ails you
What's the cure for this pain, what can one possibly do

She's exasperated and I am so keen
O lord, what might it all mean

I too have a tongue in my mouth, do ask me pray
What's it, that I'm yearning to say

We expect faithfulness from them in return
Who know not what it is, have no concern

Do good, and you'll have good too
What else can a mendicant say for you

I can die for you, my word for it you can take
I do not believe in merely praying for your sake

I know, It's nothing much, this wine
But if you get it free, Ghalib, it's fine

रोने से और इश्क़ में बेबाक़[1] हो गए
धोये गये हम ऐसे कि बस पाक हो गए

रुस्वा-ए-दहर[2] गो हुये, आवारगी से तुम
बारे तबीअतों के तो चालाक हो गए

कहता है कौन नाल-ए-बुलबुल[3] को, बे असर
परदे में गुल के लाख जिगर चाक हो गए

पूछे है क्या बुजूद-ओ-अदम[4] अहले शौक़ का
आप अपनी आग के ख़स-ओ-ख़ाशाक़[5] हो गए

करने गए थे उससे, तग़ाफ़ुल का हम गिला
की एक ही निगाह, कि बस ख़ाक हो गए

इस रंग से उठाई कल उसने 'असद' की लाश
दुश्मन भी जिसको देख के ग़मनाक हो गए

Rone se aur ishq mein bebaaq ho gaye
dhoye gaye hum aise ki bus paak ho gaye

Ruswa-e-dehar go huye, awargi se tum
bare tabiaton ke to chalaak ho gaye

Kehta hai kaun naal-e-bulbul ko, be asar
parde mein gul ke lakh jigar chaak ho gaye

Puchhe hai kya bujood-o-adam ahle shauq ka
aap apni aag ke khas-o-khashaak ho gaye

Karne gaye the us se, taghaphul ka hum gila
ki ek hi nigah, ki bus khaaq ho gaye

Is rung se uthai kal usne 'Asad' ki laash
dushman bhi jisko dekh ke gumnak ho gaye

---

1. साफ साफ कहने वाले 2. संसार भर में अपमानित 3. बुलबुल का आर्तनाद 4. अस्तित्व और अनस्तित्व 5. कूड़ा-करकट।

We cried in love and opened up further, thus
So well we were washed that it cleansed us

You may have become a butt of ridicule because
                              of the wander-itch
It has certainly made you smart and experience-rich

Who says the cries of the nightingale unavailing
                                          went
Beneath the flower's body, a thousand hearts were
                                          rent

Of the life and death of a lover, O ask me not
In their own fire they have been to cinders wrought

I had gone to her to complain of her indifference
                                          worst
But a single look from her reduced me to dust

He so lifted 'Asad's' corpse yesterday
That even his enemies could not their tears stay

कोई दिन, गर ज़िन्दगानी और है
अपने जी में हमने ठानी और है

आतशे-दोज़ख़ में, यह गर्मी कहाँ
सोज़े-गमहा-ए-निहानी¹ और है

बारहा देखी हैं उनकी रंजिशें²
पर कुछ अब के सर गिरानी और है

दे के ख़त, मुँह देखता है नामाबर³
कुछ तो पैग़ामे-ज़ुबानी और है

हो चुकीं, 'ग़ालिब', बलायें सब तमाम
एक मर्गे-नागहानी⁴ और है

Koi din, gar zindagani aur hai
apne ji mein humne thani aur hai

Aatshe-dozakh mein, yeh garmi kahan
soze-gamha-e-nihani aur hai

Baraha dekhi hain unki ranjishe
par kuchh ab ke sir girani aur hai

De ke khat, munha dekhta hai namabar
kuchh to paighame-zubani aur hai

Ho chukin, 'Ghalib', balayen sub tamam
ek marge-naghaani aur hai

---

1. आन्तरिक संताप की जलन 2. अप्रसन्नता 3. पत्र वाहक 4. अचानक आने वाली मृत्यु

If a little longer this life I find
I have other ideas in my mind

Hell fires do not contain a shred of that heat
Which can with the suffering of a heart compete

Her so often annoyed I find
But this time, the anger is of a different kind

The messenger hands over the letter and still my
face doth see
Surely, there is something more to convey orally

All other calamities have been part of my fate
A sudden death, Ghalib, now I await

जहाँ तेरा नक़्शे-क़दम देखते हैं
ख़ियाबां ख़ियाबां' इरम² देखते हैं।

तिरे सर्व क़ामत से, इक कद्दे-आदम
क़यामत के फ़ितने³ को कम देखते हैं

तमाशा कर ऐ महवे-आईनादारी⁴
तुझे किस तमन्ना से हम देखते हैं

बना कर फ़क़ीरों का हम भेस, 'ग़ालिब'
तमाशा-ए-अहले-करम⁵ देखते हैं

Jahan tera nakshe-qadam dekhte hain
khiyaban khiyaban iram dekhte hain

Tiray surve qamat se, ik kadde-aadam
qayamat ke fitne ko kum dekhte hain

Tamasha kar ai mehve-aainadari
tujhe kis tamanna se hum dekhte hain

Bana kar fakiron ka hum bhase 'Ghalib'
Tamasha-e-ahle-karam dekhte hain

---

1 क्यारी-क्यारी 2. स्वर्गोद्घान शद्दाद का बना हुआ कृत्रिम स्वर्ग 3. उपद्रव 4. आत्म श्रृंगार में लीन 5. कृपालुओं का तमाशा

On whichever pathway your footprints be
A garden of Eden there I see

Considering the nature in your stately stature
Hell's fury itself is a minor creature

Look at us, you who so intently your make-up do
With what longing we look at you

In the guise of a fakir, Ghalib, I espy
The deeds of people, generous and high

दाइम¹ पड़ा हुआ तिरे दर पर नहीं हूँ मैं
ख़ाक ऐसी ज़िन्दगी पे, कि पत्थर नहीं हूँ मैं

क्यों गर्दिशे-मुदाम² से घबरा न जाए दिल
इंसान हूँ पियाल-ओ-साग़र नहीं हूँ मैं

या रब, ज़माना मुझको मिटाता है किसलिए
लौहे-जहाँ³ पे हर्फ़े-मुकर्रर⁴ नहीं हूं मैं

किस वास्ते अज़ीज़ नहीं जानते मुझे
लालो-जमुरुदो-ज़रो-गौहर⁵ नहीं हूँ मैं

'ग़ालिब' वज़ीफ़ा ख़्वार⁶ हो, दो शाह को दुआ
वो दिन गए कि कहते थे, नौकर नहीं हूँ मैं

Daaim para hua tirey dar pir nahin hoon main
khaaq aisi zindagi pe, ki patthar nahin hoon main

Kyon gardishe-mudaam se ghabra na jaye dil
insaan hoon piyal-o-sagar nahin hoon main

Yaa rub, zamana mujhko mitata hai kisliye
Lohe-jahan pe herfe-muqarrar nahin hoon main

Kis vaste aziz nahin jante mujhe
lalo-jamurrudo-zaro-gauhar nahin hoon main

'Ghalib' wazifa khwar ho, do shah ko dua
woh din gaye ki kehte the, naukar nahin hoon main

---

1. सदैव 2. सदा की चिन्ता 3. संसार रूपी पृष्ठ 4. पुनः लिखा हुआ शब्द 5. लाल, पन्ना, सोना और मोती 6. वृत्ति पाने वाले

Would that I were lying on your doorstep prone
Fie on this life, that I am not fated to be a stone

Weary of these wanderings I'm bound to be
A human being after all, I'm not a cup and a bottle,
prithee

O God, why should the world want me to obliterate
I am not a twice-written word on the universal slate

Why won't my dear ones know me, for I am
Neither a ruby, nor gold, nor a rare gem

You are his liege Ghalib, so bless the king
Gone are the days when you could say, you are not
serving

रहिये अब ऐसी जगह चलकर, जहाँ कोई न हो
हम-सुखन कोई न हो और हम-जुबां कोई न हो

बेदरो-दीवार-सा इक घर बनाया चाहिए
कोई हमसाया¹ न हो और पासबां² कोई न हो

पड़िये ग़र बीमार, तो कोई न हो तीमारदार³
और अगर मर जाइए, तो नौहाख़्वाँ⁴ कोई न हो

Rahiye ab aisi jagah chalkar, jahan koi na ho
hum-sukhan koi na ho aur hum-zuban koi na ho

Bedaro-deewar-sa ik ghar banaya chahiye
koi humsaya na ho aur passban koi na ho

Padiye gar bimaar, to koi na ho timardaar
aur agar mar jaiye, to nauhakhawan koi na ho

---

1. पड़ोसी 2. प्रहरी 3. परिचायक 4. रोने वाला।

Let us go and live at a place now where nobody goes
Where there's none to speak to us, nobody our
language knows

Sans door, sans wall, a house should be built where
There is nobody to look after us, no neighbour there

If I fall ill there should be none to nurse me back to
health
And if I die, none at all to mourn my death

हुई ताख़ीर तो कुछ बाइसे ताख़ीर[1] भी था
आप आते थे, मगर कोई इनांगीर[2] भी था

तुम से बेजा, है मुझे अपनी तबाही का गिला
इसमें कुछ शायब-ए-ख़ूबि-ए-तक़दीर[3] भी था

तू मुझे भूल गया हो तो पता बतला दूँ
कभी फ़ितराक[4] में तेरे, कोई नख़चीर[5] भी था

क़ैद में, है तिरे वहशी को, वही जुल्फ़ की याद
हाँ कुछ इक रंजे-गिराँबारि-ए-ज़ंजीर[6] भी था

बिजली इक कौन्द गई आँखों के आगे, तो क्या
बात करते, कि मैं लब तश्न-ए-तक़रीर भी था

पकड़े जाते हैं फ़रिश्तों के लिखे पर, नाहक़
आदमी कोई हमारा, दमे-तहरीर भी था

रेख़्ते[7] के तुम्हीं उस्ताद नहीं हो 'ग़ालिब'
कहते हैं, अगले ज़माने में कोई 'मीर' भी था।

Hui takhir to kuchh baaise takhir bhi tha
aap aatey the, magar koi inangir bhi tha

Tum se beja, hai mujhe apni tabahi ka gila
isme kuchh shayab-e-khubi-e-taqdir bhi tha

Tu mujhe bhool gaya ho to pata batla doon
kabhi fitrak mein terey, koi nakhchir bhi tha

Qaid mein, hai terey vahshi ko, wahi zulf ki yaad
haan kuchh ik ranje-giranbari-e-zanzir bhi tha

Bijlee ik kaund gai aankhon ke aagey, to kya
baat karte, ki main lab tashn-e-taqrir bhi tha

Pakre jaate hain farishton ke likhe per, nahaq
aadmi koi hamara, dame-tehreer bhi tha

Rekhte ke tumhi ustaad nahin ho 'Ghalib'
Kehte hain, agley zamane mein koi 'Meer' bhi tha

---

1. देर का कारण 2. लगाम पकड़ने वाला; बाधक 3. सौभाग्य की झलक 4. शिकार या सामग्री रखने का थैला 5. शिकार की हुई चीज़ 6. ज़ंजीर के भारी बोझ का दुख 7. उर्दू शायरी

You were delayed, so there was indeed a reason
for the delay
You were coming, of course, but sombody
stopped you on the way

For my ruination, I cannot put the blame justly on you
My destiny too had in it much to do

If you have forgotten me, may I remind you, and say
I am the very same who was once in your bag of prey

In the prison too, your lover remained in your tresses
chained
Of course, there was a little weight in the shackles
also, which pained

I had been blinded by your sight like a lightning
flash, it is true
But you should have talked to me, because I was
dying to speak to you

We are punished unjustly for what the angels have done
Ignoring the fact that when our fate was written we
were represented by none

There was, they say, in the olden days a certain 'Meer'
too
You alone are not the master, Ghalib, of poetry
in Urdu

हर एक बात पे कहते हो तुम, कि तू क्या है
तुम्हीं कहो कि यह अन्दाज़े गुफ़्तगू क्या है

जला है जिस्म जहाँ, दिल भी जल गया होगा
कुरेदते हो जो अब राख, जुस्तजू क्या है

रगों में दौड़ने फिरने के, हम नहीं क़ाइल
जब आँख ही से न टपका, तो फिर लहू क्या है

रही न ताक़ते-गुफ़्तार¹ और अगर हो भी
तो किस उमीद पे कहिये कि आरजू क्या है

हुआ है शह का मुसाहिब² फिरे है इतराता
वगरना. शहर में ग़ालिब की आबरू³ क्या है।

Her ek baat pe kehte ho tum, ki tu kya hai
tumhin kaho ki yeh andaze guft⁺goo kya hai

Jala hai zism jahan, dil bhi jal gaya hoga
quredate ho jo ab raakh, justjoo kya hai

Ragon mein daurne phirne ke, hum nahin qaail
jab aankh hi se na tapka, to phir lahoo kya hai

Rahi na taqkte-guftaar aur agar ho bhi
to kis ummid pe kahiye ki aarzoo kya hai

Hua hai sheh ka musahib phirey hai itraata
vagarna shahar mein Ghalib ki Aabroo kya hai

---

1. बात करने की शक्ति 2. सभासद 3. प्रतिष्ठा

74

Everytime I speak thou sayest, what are you
Is this the way to hold conversation, let you
                                        honestly say

When the body is burnt, the heart must be burnt too
What for do you scratch the ashes, what do you want
                                        to do

It is not our wont to flow through the veins
How is it blood, if not from the eyes it rains

No strength to converse is left, and even if it
                                        were there
On what hope do I say what I desire

But a king's courtier, he struts up and down
Otherwise who cares for Ghalib in the town

हम से खुल जाओ, बवक़्ते मै परस्ती¹, एक दिन
वरना हम छेड़ेंगे, रख कर उज़्रे-मस्ती एक दिन

ग़र्रा-ए-औजे-बिना-ए-आलमे-इम्काँ² न हो
इस बुलन्दी के नसीबों में है पस्ती, एक दिन

क़र्ज़ की पीते थे मै, लेकिन समझते थे, कि हाँ
रंग लाएगी हमारी फ़ाक़ा मस्ती, एक दिन

नग़माहा-ए-ग़म³ को भी, ऐ दिल ग़नीमत जानिए
बेसदा हो जाएगा, ये साज़े-हस्ती एक दिन

धौल धप्पा उस सरापा नाज़ का⁴ शेवा नहीं
हम ही कर बैठे थे, 'ग़ालिब' पेश दस्ती⁵ एक दिन

Hum se khul jao, bawaqte mai parasti, ek din
varna hum chherenge, rakh kar ujre-masti ek din

Gharra-e-auje-bina-e-aalme-imkan na ho
is bulandi ke nasibon mein hai pasti, ek din

Karz ki peete the mai, lekin samajhte the, ki haan
rung laayegi hamari phaqa masti, ek din

Nagmaha-e-ghum ko bhi, ai dil ghanimat janiye
Besada ho jayega, ye saaze-hasti ek din

Dhaul dhappa us sarapaa naaz ka sheva nahin
hum hi kar baithe the, 'Ghalib' pesh dasti ek din

---

1. मदिरापान के समय 2. यह गर्व कि संसार अत्यन्त महान है 3. वेदना के गीत 4. गर्व की मूर्ति 5. पहल करना

Open out with us at booze one of these days please
Or else under the plea of drunkenness we are going
to tease

Don't be proud of these buildings, mighty and tall
These heights are one day destined to fall

I drank on credit, but always knew
That my recklessness will one day some mischief do

Take it as a blessing, even this song of sorrow
For the life's music may fall silent as early as
tomorrow

To come to blows was not the wont of that
beauteous one
One of these days, Ghalib, only we had an excess
done

तस्कीं को हम न रोयें, जो ज़ौक़े-नज़र[1] मिले
हूराने-ख़ुल्द[2] में तिरी सूरत मगर मिले

अपनी गली में, मुझको न कर दफ़्न, बादे-क़त्ल
मेरे पते से ख़ल्क़ को क्यों तेरा घर मिले

साक़ी गरी की शर्म करो आज, वरना हम
हर शब पिया ही करते हैं मै, जिस क़दर मिले

तुझसे तो कुछ कलाम नहीं, लेकिन ऐ नदीम[3]
मेरा सलाम कहियो, अगर नामाबर मिले

तुमको भी हम दिखायें, कि मजनूं ने क्या किया
फ़ुर्सत कशाकशे-ग़मे-पिनहाँ[4] से गर मिले

ऐ   साकिनाने-कूच-ए-दिलदार[5]   देखना
तुमको कहीं जो 'ग़ालिबे'-आशुफ़्ता सर[6] मिले

Taskin ko hum na royen, jo zokey-nazar miley
hurane-khuld mein tiri surat magar miley

Apni gali mein, mujhko na kar dafan, bade-qatal
mere patey se khalq ko kyon tera ghar miley

Saaqi gari ki sharm karo aaj, varna hum
her shab piya hi karte hain mai, jis qadar miley

Tujhse to kuchh kalam nahin, lekin ai nadim
mera salaam kahiyo, agar namabar miley

Tumko bhi hum dikhayen, ki majnu ne kya kiya
phursata kashakashe-ghamey-pinhan se gar miley

Ai sakinaney-kooch-e-dildaar dekhna
tumko kahin jo 'Ghalibe'-aashufta sir miley

---

1. दृष्टि की अभिरुचि (माशूक की सूरत जिससे दृष्टि की अभिरुचि पूरी हो सके) 2. स्वर्ग की
अप्सराएँ 3. साथी; मित्र 4. आन्तरिक दुखों की खेंचा-तानी 5. माशूक की गली में बसने
वालो 6. सरफिरा ग़ालिब।

If our eyes are gratified we look for no other
solace
Provided among the fairies of heaven we meet
your face

Bury me not, post assassination, in your street
Why should the world know your address from my
retreat

We of course drink everyday for whatever it may take
But have some shame today for at least your
Saqihood'sake

I have nothing to talk to you, O comrade dear
But do convey my compliment if you meet the
messenger

If ever I win reprieve from the sorrows of my heart
I will excel what Majnu did in every part

O you, who live in my love's street
Watch out if somewhere Ghalib the madcap you meet

हुस्न ग़म्ज़े की कशाकश¹ से छुटा मेरे बाद
बारे, आराम से है अहले-जफ़ा², मेरे बाद

मंसबे-शेफ़्तिगी³ के कोई क़ाबिल न रहा
हुई माज़ूलि-ए-अन्दाज़ो-अदा⁴ मेरे बाद

शम्अ बुझती है, तो उसमें से धुआँ उठता है
शोल-ए-इश्क़ सियह पोश हुआ मेरे बाद

ग़म से मरता हूँ कि इतना नहीं दुनिया में कोई
कि करे ताज़ियते-मेहरो-वफ़ा⁵ मेरे बाद

आये है बेकसि-ए-इश्क़⁶ पे रोना, 'ग़ालिब'
किसके घर जाएगा सैलाबे—बला मेरे बाद

Husan ghumze ki kashakash se chhuta mere baad
baare, aaram se hai ahley-zafa, mere baad

Mansabe-sheftigi ke koi kabil ne raha
hui mazuli-e-andazo-ada mere baad

Shamae bujhti hai, to usmein se dhuan uthta hai
shol-e-ishq siyah posh hua mere baad

Ghum se marta hun ki itna nahin duniya mein koi
ki karey taziyate-mehro-wafa mere baad

Aaye hai bakasi-e-ishq pe rona, 'Ghalib'
kiskey ghar jayega sailaab—bala mere baad

---

1. कष्ट 2. अन्याय करने वाले माशूक 3. आसक्ति का पद 4. माशूक के हाव-भाव का अपदस्थ होना 5. प्रेम तथा प्रेम निर्वाह की सांत्वना 6. प्रेम की असहायता

Beauty is spared the trouble of eye-craft, now that
I am gone
Most easily do they breathe now, the cruel lot, now
that I am gone

There's none to adorn the high state of attachment
in love
The amorous antics of my beloved are unheeded now

When the candle is put out, it leaves behind a
smoking arc
Now that I am gone, the flame of love is gone all dark

It grieves me immensely that there is none after
my death
To condole for love and fidelity on their loss of
breath

At this helplessness of love, Ghalib, I feel like crying
O where will the flood of misery go, now that I am
dying.

इश्क़ मुझको नहीं, वहशत ही सही
मेरी वहशत, तेरी शोहरत ही सही

क़तअ कीजे न, तअल्लुक़ हम से
कुछ नहीं है, तो अदावत ही सही

हम भी दुश्मन तो नहीं हैं अपने
ग़ैर को तुझसे मुहब्बत ही सही

हम कोई तर्क-ए-वफ़ा करते हैं
न सही इश्क़, मुसीबत ही सही

यार से छेड़ चली जाए, 'असद'
गर नहीं वस्ल¹ तो हसरत ही सही।

Ishq mujhko nahin, vehshat hi sahi
meri vahshat, teri shohrat hi sahi

Qatae kijay na, tealluk hum se
kuchh nahin hai, to adavat hi sahi

Hum bhi dushman to nahin hain apne
Ghair ko tujhse muhabbat hi sahi

Hum koi tark-e-wafa karte hain
na sahi ishq, musibat hi sahi

Yaar se chher chali jaye, 'Asad'
gar nahin vasal to hasrat hi sahi

---

1. मिलन

82

If not love, let madness be its name
Let my madness be your fame

Break not all ties with me, prithee
If nothing else between us, let at least enmity be

Even if my enemy is your lover
I am not my own enemy either

I am not the one who will his fealty abjure
Let it be a calamity, if it is love no more

Persist with your amours, 'Asad' for the friend
Even if you can't meet, let not the longing end

इशरते-क़तरा[1] है दरिया में फ़ना हो जाना
दर्द का हद से गुज़रना है दवा हो जाना

तुझसे, क़िस्मत में मिरी, सूरते-क़ुफ़्ले-अबजद[2]
था लिखा, बात के बनते ही जुदा हो जाना

अब जफ़ा से भी हैं महरूम हम, अल्ला अल्लाह
इस क़दर दुश्मने-अरबाबे-वफ़ा[3] हो जाना

ज़ोफ़[4] से, गिरिया, मुबद्दल ब दमे-सर्द[5] हुआ
वावर आया हमें पानी का हवा हो जाना

है मुझे, अब्रे-बहारी का बरस कर खुलना
रोते-रोते ग़मे-फ़ुर्कत में, फ़ना हो जाना

बख़्शे है जल्व-ए-गुल ज़ौक़े-तमाशा 'ग़ालिब'
चश्म को चाहिए हर रंग में वा हो जाना

Ishratey-qatra hai dariya mein fana ho jana
dard ka hud se guzarna hai dawa ho jana

tujhse, qismat mein miri, surate-qufley-abjad
Tha likha, baat ke bante hi juda ho jana

Ab jafa se bhi hain mehroom hum, allaa-allaah
is qadar dushmane-arbabey-wafa ho jana

Zoaf se, giriya, mubaddal be damey-sarde hua
vavar aaya hamein paani ka hawa ho jana

Hai mujhe, abrey-bahari ka baras kar khulna
rote-rote ghamey-furqat mein, fana ho jana

Bakshe hai zalv-e-gul zaukey-tamasha 'Ghalib'
chashm ko chahiye har rung mein waa ho jana

---

1. बूँद का ऐश्वर्य 2. अक्षरों के मेल से खुलने वाले ताले की भाँति 3. प्रेम निर्वाह करने वालों का शत्रु 4. निर्बलता 5. ठण्डी आह में परिवर्तित।

Glory of a drop lies in dissolving itself in the ocean
After a point, sorrows become their own solution

As a number lock opens instantly on right combination
Similarly, after all was well, my fate was separation

O God, even of her cruelty I am deprived
So much is her lover now by her despised

As I see a doleful tear turn into a soulful sigh, in
my state of infirmity
I am convinced of the veracity of the evaporation
theory

After the spring rain, the clearing up of the sky
Is, after a long weeping in separation, to die

The loveliness of flower, O Ghalib, invites us all to
enjoy the sight
The eye should always remain open and bright

जौर[1] से बाज़ आएँ, पर बाज़ आए क्या
कहते हैं, हम तुम को मुँह दिखलाएँ क्या

रात दिन गर्दिश में हैं सात आस्माँ
हो रहेगा कुछ न कुछ, घबरायें क्या

लाग हो तो उसको हम समझें लगाव
जब न हो कुछ भी, तो धोखा खायें क्या

उम्र भर देखा किये मरने की राह
मर गए पर देखिए, दिखलायें क्या

पूछते हैं वो कि 'ग़ालिब' कौन है
कोई बतलाओ कि हम बतलायें क्या

Jaur se baaz aayen, par baaz aaye kya
kehte hain, hum tum ko munha dikhlayen kya

Raat din gardish mein hain saat aasmaan
ho rahega kuchh na kuchh, ghabrayen kya

Laag ho to usko hum samjhen lagaav
jab na ho kuchh bhi, to dhokha khayen kya

Umre bhar dekha kiye marne ki raah
mar gaye par dekhiye, dikhlayen kya

Puchhte hain woh ki 'Ghalib' kaun hai
koi batlao ki hum batlaen kya

---

1. अन्याय व अत्याचार

She would refrain from cruelty, can she do so?
She says, how can she otherwise, her face show

The seven skies are turning night and day
Why worry, something has to happen, any way

If there's friction even, some attachment we can
imagine,
How can we deceive ourselves when there is none

All my life I have waited for death impatiently
Now that I am dead, let me see what shows He

Who is Ghalib he wants to know
Tell us pray, what do we say!

लाज़िम था कि देखो मेरा रस्ता कोई दिन और
तन्हा गए क्यों अब रहो तन्हा कोई दिन और

आये हो कल, और आज ही कहते हो कि जाऊँ
माना, कि हमेशा नहीं अच्छा, कोई दिन और

जाते हुए कहते हो, क़यामत को मिलेंगे
क्या खूब, क़यामत का है गोया कोई दिन और

तुम माहे-शबे-चारदहम[1] थे, मिरे घर के
फिर क्यों न रहा घर का वो नक़्शा कोई दिन और

तुम कौन से थे ऐसे खरे दादो-सितद[2] के
करता मलकुल-मौत[3] तक़ाज़ा, कोई दिन और

नादां हो, जो कहते हो, कि क्यों जीते हो 'ग़ालिब'
क़िस्मत में है, मरने की तमन्ना कोई दिन और

Laazim tha ki dekho mera rasta koi din aur
tanha gaye kyon ab raho tanha koi din aur

Aaye ho kal, aur aaj hi kehte ho ki jaaun
mana, ki hamesha nahin achha, koi din aur

Jaate huye kehte ho, qayamat ko milengay
kya khoob, qayamat ka hai goya koi din aur

Tum mahe-shabe-chardeham the, mire ghar ke
phir kyon na raha ghar ka woh naqsha koi din aur

Tum kaun se the aise khare dado-sitad ke
karta malkul-maut taqaza koi din aur

Nadaan ho, jo kehte ho, ki kyon jitey ho 'Ghalib'
qismat mein hai, marne ki tamanna koi din aur

---

1. चौदहवीं रात का चाँद 2. लेन-देन 3. यमराज

You ought to have waited for me a few days more
You went alone, so let you alone be a few days more

You came just yesterday, and would like to go today
Not for ever though, a little longer let you stay

As you go, we will meet on the day of judgement
you say
As if for the judgement there is going to be some
other day

A full waxing moon for my house you were
Then why did you not shine a little longer

You were not so holy in your dealings, I'm sure
Couldn't you have put off the angel of death for a
few days more?

You are naive that you ask Ghalib why he is living still,
To yearn a little longer for death is destiny's will

मैं उन्हें छेड़ूँ और कुछ न कहें
चल निकलते, जो मै पिए होते

कहर हो या बला हो, जो कुछ हो
काश के, तुम मिरे लिए होते

मेरी क़िस्मत में ग़म गर इतना था
दिल भी, या रब कई दिये होते

आ ही जाता वो राह पर, 'ग़ालिब'
कोई दिन और भी जिए होते

Main unhen chherun aur kuchh na kahen
chal nikalte, jo mai piye hote

Qahar ho ya bala ho, jo kuchh ho
kash ke, tum mire liye hote

Meri qismat mein ghum gar itna tha
dil bhi, yaa rub kai diye hote

Aa hi jata woh raah par, 'Ghalib'
koi din aur bhi jiye hote

I tease her, and she protests not
Would God, I were a drunken lot

Cruel or callous, whatever you be
How I wish, you were for me only

If so much sorrow was my lot
O God, I should have been given more than one heart

He would have, O Ghalib, come around
If only a little more life you had found

बस कि दुश्वार है, हर काम का आसां होना
आदमी को भी मुयस्सर नहीं इन्सां होना

गिरिया चाहे है ख़राबी मिरे काशाने¹ की
दरो-दीवार से टपके है, बयाबां होना

वाए दीवानगी-ए-शौक़², कि हरदम मुझको
आप जाना उधर, और आप ही हैरां होना

की मिरे क़त्ल के बाद, उसने जफ़ा से तौबा
हाय, उस ज़ूद पशेमां का पशेमां होना

हैफ़³ उस चार गिरह कपड़े की क़िस्मत, 'ग़ालिब'
जिसकी क़िस्मत में हो, आशिक़ का गरीबां होना

Bus ki dushwar hai, her kaam ka aasaan hona
aadmi ko bhi muyassar nahin insaan hona

Giriya chahe hai kharabi mire kashaane ki
daro-deewar se tapke hai, bayabaan hona

Wae diwangi-e-shauq, ki herdum mujhko
aap jana udhar, aur aap he hairan hona

Ki mire qatal ke baad, usne japha se tauba
haae, us zood pasheman ka pasheman hona

Haif us chaar girah kapre ki qismat, 'Ghalib'
jiskee qismat mein ho, aashiq ka gariban hona

---

1. घर 2. प्यार का पागलपन 3. धिक्कार

It is hard indeed for anything to be easy
Even humans have yet to attain humanity

Destruction of my house is the wish of this
                                    lamentation
The walls and the windows are already a picture of
                                    desolation

What madness in love that everytime I myself decide
To go there, and everytime, at my folly feel surprised

After murdering me, never to be cruel, she vows
O the repentance of one who so quick a repentance
                                    shows

Fie, Ghalib, on that four inches of cloth
Whose fate is to cover a lover's chest and throat

यह हम जो हिज्र में, दीवारो-दर को देखते हैं
कभी सबा को, कभी नामाबर' को देखते हैं

वो आयें घर में हमारे, ख़ुदा की क़ुदरत है
कभी हम उनको, कभी अपने घर को देखते हैं

नज़र लगे न कहीं, उसके दस्तो-बाज़ू² को
ये लोग क्यों मेरे ज़ख़्मे-जिगर को देखते हैं

तिरे जवाहिरे-तफ़्रें-कुलह³ को क्या देखें
हम औजे-ताले-ए-लालो-गुहर⁴ को देखते हैं

Yeh hum jo hijra mein, dewaro-dar ko dekhte hain
kabhi saba ko, kabhi namabar ko dekhte hain

Woh aayen ghar mein hamare, khuda ki qudrat hai
kabhi hum unko, kabhi apne ghar ko dekhte hain

Nazar lagey na kahin, uske dasto-bazoo ko
ye log kyon mere zakhme-jigar ko dekhte hain

Tire zawahire-terfe-kulah ko kya dekhen
hum aujey-tale-e-laalo-guhar ko dekhte hain

1. संदेशवाहक 2. हाथ और भुजाएँ 3. टोपी में टंके हुए रत्न 4. हीरे मोती के भाग्य की ऊँचाई।

In hours of separation, at the wall we stare, towards
the door we bend,
Look for the courier, to the morning breeze our
ear lend

He comes to our house, God shows his grace
We sometime look at him, sometime at our place

May God, save her hand and arm from evil eye
Why do these people my wounded heart espy

I admire not so much the jewel in your crown
I marvel instead at the stone's fortune

हवस को है नशाते-कार¹ क्या क्या
न हो मरना तो जीने का मज़ा क्या

नवाज़िशहा-ए-बेज़ा² देखता हूँ
शिकायतहा-ए-रंगीं का गिला क्या

निगाहे-बेमहाबा³ चाहता हूँ
तग़ाफुलहा-ए-तसकीं⁴ आज़मा क्या

दिले-हर क़तरा है साजे-अनल बहर
हम उसके हैं, हमारा पूछना क्या

बला-ए-जां है, 'ग़ालिब', उसकी हर बात
इबारत क्या, इशारत क्या, अदा क्या

Havas ko hai nashate-kaar kya kya
na ho marna to jiney ka maza kya

Navazishaha-e-beza dekhta hoon
shikaytaha-e-rangi ka gila kya

Nigahe-bemahaba chahata hun
taghafulha-e-taskin aazma kya

Diley-her qatra hai saaze-anal beher
hum uske hain, hamara puchhna kya

Bala-e-jaan hai, 'Ghalib', uski her baat
Ibarat kya, isharat kya, ada kya

Lust and desire delight in deeds of various kind
If there were no death, life would not any joy find

Undue favours to my rival, I see
If I complain amorously, why should resent she

Full and free glances from her I desire
Why should indifference test my patience, and me
so tire

The heart of every drop is the music of ocean
We belong to Him, what is it then that we do not keep

O Ghalib, everything about her is murderous
Be it her style, her form, her gesture

वो आके ख़्वाब में तस्कीने-इज़्तिराब' तो दे
वले मुझे तपिशे-दिल* मजाले-ख़्वाब* तो दे

करे है क़त्ल लगावट में तेरा रो देना
तिरी तरह कोई तेग़े-निगह का आब तो दे

पिला दे ओक से साक़ी, जो हमसे नफ़रत है
पियाला गर नहीं देता, न दे, शराब तो दे

'असद' ख़ुशी से मेरे हाथ पाँव फूल गए
कहा जो उसने, ज़रा मेरे पाँव दाब तो दे

Woh Aakey khwab mein taskine-iztiraab to de
vale mujhe tapishe-dil majale-khwab to de

Karey hai qatal lagawat mein tera ro dena
tiri tarah koi teghey-nigah ka aab to de

Pila de oak se saaqi, jo humse nafrat hai
piyala gar nahin deta, na de, sharaab to de

'Asad' khushi se mere haath paon phool gaye
kaha jo usne, zara mere paon daab to de

---

1. व्याकुलता में सांत्वना 2. मन की तपन 3. सोने का साहस

Let her come in my dream, and me from restlessness
                                    redeem
But, before that, let my heart's turmoil give me
                        peace to sleep and dream

Your tearful eye in love is a ravishing sight
Who else will have a glance so murderous and bright

You may not give us the cup, O Saqi, if unworthy you
                                    think
We'll cup our palm, but pray give us the drink

As she asked me, 'Asad', to press her feet
I was beyond myself with joy's surfeit

दिल से तिरी निगाह जिगर तक उतर गई
दोनों को इक अदा में रज़ामन्द कर गई

वो बाद-ए-शबाना' की सरमस्तियां कहाँ
उठिये बस अब, कि लज़्ज़ते-ख़्वाबे-सहर² गई

उड़ती फिरे है ख़ाक मिरी, कू-ए-यार में
बारे अब ऐ हवा, हवसे-बालो-पर गई

देखो तो, दिल फ़रेबि-ए-अन्दाज़े-नक़्शे-पा³
मौजे-ख़िरामे-यार⁴ भी, क्या गुल कतर गई

नज़्ज़ारे ने भी, काम किया वां निक़ाब का
मस्ती से हर निगह तिरे रुख़ पर बिखर गई

मारा ज़माने ने, 'असदुल्ला खां' तुम्हें
वो वलवले⁵ कहाँ, वो जवानी किधर गई

Dil se tiri nigaah jigar tak utar gai
dono ko ik ada mein razamand kar gai

Woh baad-e-shabana ki sirmastiyan kahan
uthiye bus ab, ki lazzate-khwabe-sahar gai

Urti phire hai khaaq miri, ku-e-yaar mein
Baare ab ai hawa, havse-balo-par gai

Dekho to, dil pharebi-e-andaze-naqshe-pa
mauje-khirame-yaar bhi, kya gul katar gai

Nazzarey ne bhi, kaam kiya waan niqab ka
masti se her nigah tirey rukh par bikhar gai

Maara zamane ne, 'Asadullah khan' tumhen
woh valvaley kahan, woh jawani kidhar gai

---

1. रात्रि की मदिरा (यौवन की रात्रि से तथा वृद्धावस्था की सुबह से उपमा दी जाती है)
2. प्रातःकालीन निद्रा का आनन्द 3. पदचिह्न की मनमोहकता 4. मित्र (माशूक़) की
मंथरगति की तरंग 5. उमंगें

100

Your lovely glance pierces my heart and head
                                        through
And makes them both your bidding do

Intoxication of youth gone, all gone
Awake, for it's over now, the lovely dream of dawn

My dust is blowing around in my love's lane thick
                                        and fast
All my desire to fly in the air is quenched at last

How lovely are the foot-prints of my beloved there
As she sallies around, she strews flowers everywhere

Even the sight acted as screen in this case
In sheer ecstasy the gaze was spread on your face

Times have undone you O Asadullah Khan
Where is that spark now, where's the youth gone

दोस्त, ग़मख़्वारी में मेरी, सइ फ़रमायेंगे क्या
ज़ख़्म के भरने तलक, नाखुन न बढ़ जायेंगे क्या

बेनियाज़ी' हद से गुज़री, बन्दा परवर कब तलक
हम कहेंगे हाले-दिल, और आप फ़रमायेंगे क्या

हज़रते-नासेह गर आयें, दीद-ओ-दिल फ़र्शे-राह
कोई मुझको यह तो समझा दो, कि समझायेंगे क्या

गर किया नासेह ने हमको क़ैद, अच्छा, यूँ सही
ये जुनूने-इश्क़ के अन्दाज़ छुट जाएँगे क्या

है अब इस मामूरे³ में केहते-ग़मे उल्फ़त², 'असद'
हमने यह माना, कि दिल्ली में रहें, खायेंगे क्या

Dost, ghumkhwari mein meri, sai pharmayenge kya
zakhm ke bharne talak, nakhun na badh jayenge kya

Beniyazi hud se guzari, banda parvar kab talak
hum kahenge haale-dil, aur aap pharmayenge kya

Hazratey-naaseh gar aayen, deed-o-dil farshe-raah
koi mujhko yeh to samjha do, ki samjhayenge kya

Gar kiya naaseh ne humko qaid, achha, yun sahi
ye junoone-ishq ke andaaz chhoot jayenge kya

Hai ab is mamurey mein kehte-ghamey ulfat, 'Asad'
humne yeh mana, ki dilli mein rahen, khayenge kya

---

1. निस्पृहता 2. बस्ती 3. प्रेम के दुखों का अकाल

How would my friends help if sympathy they had
shown
By the time the wound healed, would not the nails
have once again grown

Indifference crosses all limits, how far, O master dear
I'll tell you my plight and you'll, pretend not to hear

If the preacher comes I'll welcome him most heartily
But will somebody say what he can possibly tell me

If the preacher has sent me behind bars, I harbour
no ill-will
But can he quell my love's frenzy still

It's love's famine 'Asad' that you in this city meet
Granted, we shall live in Delhi, but what shall we eat

न हुई ग़र मिरे मरने से तसल्ली न सही
इम्तिहाँ और भी बाक़ी हों, तो ये भी न सही

एक हंगामे पे मौक़ूफ़[1] है घर की रौनक़
नौहा-ए-ग़म[2] ही सही, नग़्मा-ए-शादी न सही

न सताइश[3] की तमन्ना, न सिले[4] की परवाह
ग़र नहीं हैं मेरे अश्आर में मायने, न सही

इशरत-ए-सोहबते-ख़ूबाँ[5] ही ग़नीमत समझो
न हुई 'ग़ालिब' अगर उम्र-ए-तबेई न सही

Na hui gar mire marne se tasalli na sahi
Imtihaan aur bhi baaki hon, to ye bhi na sahi

Ek hungame pe mauquf hai ghar ki raunak
nauha-e-ghum hi sahi, nagma-e-shadi na sahi

Na sataish ki tamanna, na silay ki parvah
gar nahin hain mere ashaar mein mani, na sahi

Ishrat-e-sohbate-khooban hi ganimat samjho
na hui 'Ghalib' agar umre-e-tabai na sahi

---

1. ठहरा हुआ 2. दुःख का विलाप 3. प्रशंसा 4. इनाम 5. अच्छे लोगों का संग

If she is not satisfied even with my life's sacrifice
Let her give me another test, if this one doesn't suffice

Liveliness in the house needs noises lively and strong
Let it be the notes of a dirge, if not a wedding song

I desire not praise, nor a reward I seek
Let it be so, if my poetry is all Greek

The company of the charming people, Ghalib, is a
great blessing
Then even if life is short, it is a minor thing

कोई उम्मीद बर नहीं आती
कोई सूरत नज़र नहीं आती

मौत का एक दिन मुऐयेन[1] है
नींद क्यों रात भर नहीं आती

आगे आती थी हाले-दिल पे हंसी
अब किसी बात पर नहीं आती

है कुछ ऐसी ही बात, जो चुप हूँ
वरना क्या बात कर नहीं आती

हम वहाँ हैं जहाँ से हमको भी
कुछ हमारी ख़बर नहीं आती

मरते हैं आरज़ू में मरने की
मौत आती है पर नहीं आती

काबा किस मुँह से जाओगे 'ग़ालिब'
शर्म तुमको मगर नहीं आती

Koi ummid bar nahin aati
koi surat nazar nahin aati

Maut ka ek din mueyen hai
nind kyon raat bhar nahin aati

Aage aati thi haale-dil pe hansi
ab kisi baat par nahin aati

Hai kuchh aisee hi baat, jo chup hoon
varna kya baat kar nahin aati

Hum wahan hain jahan se humko bhi
kuchh hamari khabar nahin aati

Marte hain aarzoo mein marne ki
maut aati hai par nahin aati

Kaba kis munha se jaogey 'Ghalib'
sharm tumko magar nahin aati

---

1. निश्चित

106

No hope, no light
Not a way out seems in sight

The day of our death is fixed alright
Why keep we then awake all night

Earlier my heart could beguile me a while
Now, nothing can make me smile

Something it is that keeps me quiet, aye
Otherwise what is it that I cannnot say

I am at a place where about myself too
I hardly ever get a clue

How I wish, I could die
Death comes not, it passes by

How could you have the cheek, Ghalib, to do a
pilgrimage to Kaba
But shame is perhaps the last thing to have
touched you

शौक़ हर रंग, रक़ीबे-सरो-सामां[1] निकला
क़ैस तस्वीर के पर्दे में भी उरियां निकला

ज़ख़्म ने दाद न दी तंगि-ए-दिल की या रब
तीर भी सीन-ए-बिस्मिल से परअफ़शां[2] निकला

बू-ए-गुल, नाल-ए-दिल, दूदे-चराग़े-महफ़िल[3]
जो तिरी बज़्म से निकला, सो परीशां निकला

चन्द तस्वीरे-बुतां, चंद हसीनों के खतूत
बाद मरने के मेरे घर से ये सामां निकला

दिल में फिर गिरिए ने जोर उठाया, 'ग़ालिब'
आह जो क़तरा न निकला था, सो तूफ़ां निकला

Shauq her rung, raqibe-saro-samaan nikla
Qais tasvir ke parde mein bhi uriyan nikla

Zakhm ne daad na di tangi-e-dil ki ya rub
teer bhi seen-e-bismil se parahshan nikla

Boo-e-gul, naal-e-dil, dudey-charaghey-mehfil
jo tiri bazm se nikla, so parishan nikla

Chand tasweerein-butaan, chand haseenon ke khatoot
baad marne ke mere ghar se ye samaan nikla

Dil mein phir giriye ne zor uthaya 'Ghalib'
Aah jo qatra na nikla tha, so tufan nikla

---

1. हर प्रकार की सज्जा या श्रृंगार का शत्रु 2. पर झाड़ता हुआ या परेशान 3. महफिल के दीपक का धुआं

108

Love, in any case, needs no outward trapping
Qais is naked even in the painting

Even for the narrow space in the heart, the wound
did not a favour do
Only with spread out feet, the arrow from the
wounded breast withdrew

The fragrance of the flower, the smoke from the
candle
in the hall as also lamentation of the heart
Whatever from your presence emerged, emerged
distraught

A few photographs, a few letters form the beauties
around
Is about all that after my death from the house was
found

The heart is welling up once again to cry
What appeared to be not even a drop, Ghalib is a
typhoon nigh

ये न थी हमारी क़िस्मत कि विसाले-यार होता
अगर और जीते रहते, यही इन्तिज़ार होता

तिरे वादे पर जिये हम, तो यह जान, झूट जाना
कि ख़ुशी से मर न जाते, अगर एतबार होता

कोई मेरे दिल से पूछे, तेरे तीरे-नीमकश[1] को
ये ख़लिश[2] कहाँ से होती, जो जिगर के पार होता

ये कहाँ की दोस्ती है, कि बने हैं दोस्त, नासेह
कोई चारासाज़ होता, कोई ग़मगुसार होता

ग़म अगरचे जांगुसिल[3] है पर कहाँ बचें, कि दिल है
ग़मे-इश्क़ गर न होता, ग़मे-रोज़गार होता

कहूँ किससे मैं कि क्या है, शबे-ग़म[4] बुरी बला है
मुझे क्या बुरा था मरना, अगर एक बार होता

हुए मरके हम जो रुस्वा, हुए क्यों न ग़र्के़-दरिया
न कभी जनाज़ा उठता, न कहीं मज़ार होता

ये मसाइले-तसव्वुफ़, यह तिरा बयान, 'ग़ालिब'
तुझे हम वली समझते, जो न बादाख़्वार[5] होता

Ye na thi hamari kismat ki visaley-yaar hota
agar aur jitey rehte, yahi intizaar hota

Tiray wadey par jiye hum, to yeh jaan, jhoot jana
Ki khushi se mar na jaate, agar aitbaar hota

Koi mere dil se puchhe, terey teeray-neemkash ko
ye khalish kahan se hoti, jo jigar ke paar hota

Ye kahan ki dosti hai, ki bane hain dost, naaseh
koi charasaaz hota, koi ghumgusaar hota

Ghum agrachey jaangusil hai per kahan bachen, ki dil hai
ghamey-ishq gar ne hota, ghamey-rozgaar hota

Kahun kis se main ki kya hai, shabe-ghum buri bala hai
mujhe kya bura tha marna, agar ek baar hota

Huye markey hum jo rusva, huye kyon na gharqey-dariya
ne kabhi janaza uthta, ne koi mazaar hota

Ye masailey-tasavvuf, yeh tera bayaan, 'Ghalib'
tujhe hum wali samajhte, jo na badakhwar hota

---

1. आधा खिंचा हुआ तीर 2. चुभन, वेदना 3. कष्टदायक 4. गम की रात 5. शराबी

110

It wasn't a part of my luck to meet my beloved ever
I would have only waited and waited, if I had lived longer

Trust not, my love, that I took your word for true
I would have died for joy, if I could trust you

O ask me, pray, from where your half drawn arrow got
The poignancy that it has to my heart brought

The friendliness of a preacher, what friendliness to endure
Somebody should have my grief shared, someone
should my suffering cure

In the case of the heart, how can you avoid grief
although it is life-consuming
If it were not the grief of love, it would have been
the travail of earning a living

It is a nasty thing, this nightly suffering, whom
I should tell
I would have just not cared if I had only once
to die

This disgrace would have been avoided if in a
river I was drowned
Neither would the coffin have been lifted, nor
anywhere the mausoleum found

This felicity of expression, these philosophical
dis courses great
Were you not a drinker, Ghalib, you would have
been divinity incarnate

दिल मिरा, सोज़े निहाँ[1] से, बेमहाबा[2] जल गया
आतशे-ख़ामोश की मानिंद गोया जल गया

दिल में, ज़ौक़े-वस्लो-यादे-यार[3] तक, बाक़ी नहीं
आग इस घर में लगी ऐसी, कि जो था जल गया

अर्ज़ कीजे, जौहरे-अंदेशा[4] की गर्मी कहाँ
कुछ ख़्याल आया था वहशत का, कि सहरा जल गया

दिल नहीं, तुझको दिखाता वर्ना, दाग़ों की बहार
इस चराग़ां का, करूं क्या, कारफ़रमा[5] जल गया

मैं हूँ और अफ़सुर्दगी[6] की आरज़ू, 'ग़ालिब' कि दिल
देख कर तर्ज़े-तपाके-अहले-दुनिया[7] जल गया

Dil mira, sozey nihan se, bemehaba jal gaya
aatshe-khamosh ki manind goya jal gaya

Dil mein, zauke-vaslo-yade-yaar tak, baaqi nahin
aag is ghar mein lagi aisee, ki jo tha jal gaya

Arz keejay, jauhare-andesha ki garmi kahaan
kuchh khayal aaya tha vehshat ka, ki sehra jal gaya

Dil nahin, tujhko dikhta varna, daagon ki bahaar
is charaghan ka, karoon kya, karfarma jal gaya

Main hoon aur afsurdgi ki aarzoo, 'Ghalib' ki dil
dekh kar tarze-tapake-ahle-duniya jal gaya

---

1. छिपी हुई जलन 2. बिल्कुल 3. मिलन का आनन्द तथा मित्र की स्मृति 4. चिंतन की आत्मा
5. प्रबंधक 6. कुम्लाहट 7. दुनिया वालों का आव-भगत करने का तरीका

112

Like silent fire, so to say
Most indifferently, my heart from internal heat, burnt
away

The heart is bereft even of the memory of meeting the
sweetheart
Such was the blaze in my house that it burnt
everything of every sort

Where should I go and show the jewel of my thought
The moment I think of desolation, I see the desert
in fire caught

I show you not my heart for it is full of scars and stains
What shall I do of this illumination when not even
the prime mover remains

To fade away from the world, O Ghalib, is all I desire
Its manner of hospitality has set me on fire

दर्द मिन्नतकशे-दवा' न हुआ
मैं न अच्छा हुआ, बुरा न हुआ

जमा करते हो क्यों रक़ीबों को
इक तमाशा हुआ, गिला न हुआ

हम कहाँ क़िस्मत आज़माने जायँ
तू ही जब ख़ंजर आज़माँ* न हुआ

कितने शीरीं हैं तेरे लब, कि रक़ीब
गालियां खा के बेमज़ा न हुआ

है ख़बर गर्म उनके आने की
आज ही, घर में बोरिया न हुआ

क्या वो नमरूद की ख़ुदाई थी
बन्दगी में मिरा भला न हुआ

जान दी, दी हुई उसी की थी
हक़ तो यह है कि हक़ अदा न हुआ

कुछ तो पढ़िये, कि लोग कहते हैं
आज 'ग़ालिब' ग़ज़लसरा न हुआ

Dard minnatkashe-dawa na hua
main na achha hua, bura ne hua

Jama karte ho kyon raqibon ko
ik tamasha hua, gila na hua

Hum kahan qismat aazmane jayen
tu hi jab khanzar aazmaan na hua

Kitne shireen hain terey lab, ki raqib
gaaliyan kha ke bemaza ne hua

Hai khabar garm unke aaney ki
aaj hi, ghar mein boriya ne hua

Kya woh namrood ki khudai thi
bandagi mein mira bhala na hua

Jaan di, di hui usee ki thi
haq to yeh hai ki haq ada na hua

Kuchh to pariye, ki log kehte hain
aaj 'Ghalib' gazalsara na hua

---

1. दवा का आभारी 2. खंजर चलाने वाला

114

My pain won't take obligation even from the
                    medicine's healing touch
If I am not well, it is not really much

Why do you collect my rivals, pray
Is it complaint or a fun-game, say

Where should I go and try my luck, prithee
If you too do not test your sword on me

How sweet must be your lips, indeed
That even my rival enjoyed the abuse you heaped

She is visiting our house, the news is hot
And today, we don't have a mat, O sad lot

Was it a case of Namrood's godhood
Even submission to you did me no good

I gave my life, It was His boon only
The truth is that I did not acquit myself fully

Do recite something, for the people say
Ghalib has not sung a ghazal today

ज़िक्र उस परीवश¹ का, और फिर बयां अपना
बन गया रक़ीब आखिर, था जो राज़दां अपना

मंज़र इक बुलन्दी पर, और हम बना सकते
अर्श से इधर होता काश कि मकां अपना

दे वो जिस क़दर ज़िल्लत, हम हँसी में टालेंगे
बारे आश्ना निकला, उनका पासबां अपना

दर्दे दिल लिखूँ कब तक, जाऊँ उनको दिखला दूँ
उँगलियाँ फ़िगार² अपनी, खामा³ खूंचका⁴ अपना

ता करे न गम्माज़ी⁵ कर लिया है दुश्मन को
दोस्त की शिकायत में, हमने हमज़ुबां अपना

हम कहाँ के दाना थे, किस हुनर में यक्ता थे
बे सबब हुआ 'ग़ालिब', दुश्मन आसमां अपना

Zikra us parivash ka, aur phir bayaan apna
ban gaya raqib aakhir, tha jo razdaan apna

Manjar ik bulandi par, aur hum bana sakte
arsh se idhar hota kaash ki makaan apna

De woh jis qadar zillat, hum hansi mein talengey
baare aashna nikla, unka paasbaan apna

Darde dil likhoon kab tak, jaoon unko dikhla doon
ungaliyan figaar apni, khama khunchka apna

Ta karey na gammazee kar liya hai dushman ko
dost ki shikayat mein, humne humzuban apna

Hum kahan ke daana the, kis hunar mein yakta the
we sabub hua 'Ghalib', dushman aasmaan apna

---

1. परी जैसी सुन्दर 2. घायल 3. कलम 4. जिससे रक्त टपक रहा हो 5. चुगली

One, that fairy like face, and then my rapt recital of it
Has turned into a rival, my confidant fit

There should have been a sight higher than the high
How I wish, I had a house near the sky

Whatever humiliations she heaps, I shall laugh away,
                                        what else I can
For, my confidant turns out to be her man

How long can I write of my heartache? Why not go
                          and show her then
My injured finger, my blood-stained pen

In my complaint against my sweetheart, lest he
                          should backbite me
I have made a common cause with my enemy

What art have I perfected, what wisdom won
The heavens turn against me Ghalib for no rhyme
                                      or reason

न था कुछ, तो ख़ुदा था, कुछ न होता तो ख़ुदा होता
डुबोया मुझको होने ने, न होता मैं तो क्या होता

हुआ जब ग़म से यूं बेहिस¹, तो ग़म क्या सर के कटने का
न होता गर जुदा तन से, तो जानू² पर धरा होता

हुई मुद्दत, कि 'ग़ालिब' मर गया, पर याद आता है
वो हर इक बात पर कहना, कि यूँ होता तो क्या होता

Na tha kuchh, to khuda tha, kuchh na hota to khuda hota
duboya mujhko honey ne, na hota main to kya hota

Hua jab ghum se yun behis, to ghum kya sir ke katne ka
na hota gar juda tan se, to jaanu par dhara hota

hui muddat, ki 'Ghalib' mar gaya, par yaad aata hai
woh her ik baat per kehna, ki yun hota to kya hota

---

1. स्तब्ध 2. घुटना

God existed when nothing else did, God would have
existed if nothing were there
I have been undone by my being, nothing would
have been lost if I were not here

So miserable already, why should I for the loss of my
head worry
If it had not been sundered from the body, it would
have been lying on my knee

It's ages now that Ghalib died, we still remember
though
His eternal question as to what would happen if it
were thus, if it were so

मैं, और बज़्मे-मै से यूं तश्नाकाम आऊँ
गर मैंने की थी तौबा, साक़ी को क्या हुआ था

है एक तीर, जिसमें दोनों छिदे पड़े हैं
वो दिन गए, कि अपना दिल से जिगर जुदा था

दरमान्दगी¹ में 'ग़ालिब' कुछ बन पड़े तो जानूँ
जब रिश्ता बेगिरह था, नाखुन गिरह कुशा था

Main, aur bazme-mai se yun tashnakaam aaun
gar maine ki thi tauba, saaqi ko kya hua tha

Hai ek teer, jisme dono chhiday pare hain
woh din gaye, ki apna dil se jigar juda tha

Darmandagi mein 'Ghalib' kuchh ban parey to jaanu
jab rishta begirah tha, nakhun girah kusha tha

---

1. परेशानी, कलेश

Oh, and I should come from the tavern thirsty!
If I had avowed not to drink, what had happened
to the Saqi?

Gone are the days when our heart and head were two
There's an arrow now that pierce both of them
through

O that in this plight Ghalib, I could do aught
Earlier when I could untie it, there was no knot

अर्ज़े-नियाज़े-इश्क़[1] के क़ाबिल नहीं रहा
जिस दिल पे नाज़ था मुझे, वो दिल नहीं रहा

जाता हूँ दाग़े-हसरते-हस्ती[2] लिए हुए
हूं शम्-ए-कुश्ता, दरखुरे-महफ़िल[4] नहीं रहा

मरने की, ऐ दिल और ही तदबीर कर, कि मैं
शायाने-दस्तो-बाज़ु-ए-क़ातिल[5] नहीं रहा

बर रू-ए-शश जिहत[6], दरे आईना बाज़ है
यां इम्तियाजे-नाकिसो-कामिल[7] नहीं रहा

गो मैं रहा रहीने-सितमहा-ए-रोज़गार[8]
लेकिन तिरे ख़याल से ग़ाफ़िल नहीं रहा

बेदादे-इश्क़[9] से नहीं डरता, मगर 'असद'
जिस दिल पे नाज़ था मुझे, वो दिल नहीं रहा

Arze-niyaze-ishq ke kabil nahin raha
jis dil pe naaz tha mujhe, woh dil nahin raha

jaata hun daagey-husrate-hasti liye hue
hun sham-e-kushta, darkhure-mehfil nahin raha

Marne ki, ai dil aur hi tadbeer kar, ki main
shaayane-dasto-baazu-e-qatil nahin raha

Go main raha rahine-sitmaha-e-rozgaar
lekin tirey khayal se ghafil nahin raha

Bedaday-ishq se nahin darta, magar 'Asad'
jis dil pe naaz tha mujhe, woh dil nahin raha

---

1. प्रेमाकांक्षा की अभिव्यक्ति 2. जीवनाभिलाषों का दाग 3. बुझा हुआ दीपक 4. महफिल के योग्य 5. कातिल के हाथों और भुजाओं द्वारा वध किये जाने योग्य 6. पृथ्वी तथा आकाश के मुख पर 7. पूर्ण तथा अपूर्ण का भेद 8. संसार के अत्याचार का शिकार 9. प्रेम का अत्याचार

I am no longer worthy of serving my love, alas
The heart I was proud of, is no longer the heart that
it was

Hence I go bearing scars of desire on my heart
A burnt out candle I am that the mehfil needs not

Think of some other means of dying, O my heart
now
For, I am no longer fit to die at the hands of my love

East, west, north, south, there are mirrors above and
below
The world no longer, doth the difference between
right and wrong know

Though the cruel business of life kept me
preoccupied
Not for a moment, was I forgetful of thee

'Asad', I am not discouraged by unrequited love
The heart that I was proud of is no longer that heart
now

हैरां हूँ दिल को रोऊँ, कि पीटूं जिगर को मैं
मक़दूर हों, जो साथ रखूं नौहागर को मैं

छोड़ा न रश्क ने, कि तिरे घर का नाम लूं
हर इक से पूछता हूँ, कि जाऊँ किधर को मैं

जाना पड़ा रक़ीब के दर पर, हज़ार बार
ऐ काश जानता न तिरी रहगुज़र को मैं

चलता हूँ थोड़ी दूर, हर इक तेज़ रौँ के साथ
पहचानता नहीं हूँ, अभी, राहबर को मैं

फिर बेख़ुदी में भूल गया, राहे-कू-ए-यार
जाता वगरनाँ, एक दिन अपनी ख़बर को मैं

Hairaan hun, dil ko roun, ki pitoon jigar ko main
maqdoor ho, jo saath rakhoon nauhagar ko main

Chhora ne rashq ne, ki tirey ghar ka naam loon
her ik se puchhta hun, ki jaun kidhar ko main

Jana para raqib ke dar per, hazaar baar
ai kaash jaanta ne teri rehguzar ko main

Chalta hun thori door, her ik tez rau ke saath
pehchanta nahin hun, abhi, raahbar ko main

Phir bekhudi mein bhool gaya, rahe-koo-e-yaar
jata vagarna, ek din apni khabar ko main

---

1. सामर्थ्य 2. शोक मनाने वाला 3. तीव्रगामी 4. मित्र की गली का मार्ग 5. वर्ना

124

I know not whether for my heart or head I should cry
If I could afford it, a professional mourner I would try

I dare not mention your house out of jealously
So, which way do I go, I'm asking everybody

A thousand times for help, to my rival I had to sue
How I wish, you and your way I never knew

With every journeyman quick, a few steps I go
My guide as yet I do not know

Out of forgetfulness, once again I have lost my
                                                love's lane
Otherwise, my fate to know, I would go, shine or
                                                rain

क्यों जल गया न, ताब-ए-रुख़े-यार[1] देखकर
जलता हूँ अपनी ताक़त-ए-दीदार देख कर

आतिश परस्त कहते हैं अहल-ए-जहाँ मुझे
सरगर्म-ए-नालाहा-ए-शररबार देखकर

इन आबलों से पाँव के घबरा गया था मैं
जी ख़ुश हुआ है राह को पुरख़ार[2] देखकर

सर फोड़ना वो ग़ालिबे-शोरीदा[3] हाल का
याद आ गया मुझे, तेरी दीवार देखकर

Kyon jal gaya ne, taab-e-rukhey-yaar dekhkar
jalta hun apni taaqat-e-didaar dekhkar

Aatish parast kehte hain ahal-e-jahan mujhe
sirgarm-e-nalaaha-e-shararbaar dekhkar

In aablon se paon ke ghabra gaya tha main
Ji khush hua hai raah ko purkhaar dekhkar

Sir phorna woh ghalibe-shoreeda haal ka
yaad aa gaya mujhe, teri deewar dekhkar

---

1. महबूबा के रुख की चमक 2. कांटेदार 3. परेशान

Why wasn't I burnt by the fiery charm of my beloved's
face
I am jealous even of my ability to withstand her grace

They all call me a fire-worshipper, this common crowd
For they find me shedding hot tears, crying aloud

These blisters in the feet had started bothering me
Good, that the road I walk now is thorny

As I see your wall, I perforce recall
Ghalib, the distraught breaking his head against a
wall

नो वफ़ा हमसे, तो ग़ैर उसको जफ़ा कहते हैं
होती आई है, कि अच्छों को बुरा कहते हैं

आज हम अपनी परेशानि-ए-ख़ातिर' उनसे
कहने जाते तो हैं, पर देखिए क्या कहते हैं

अगले वक़्तों के हैं ये लोग, इन्हें कुछ न कहो
जो मै-ओ-नग़्मा² को, अन्दोह रुबा³ कहते हैं

देखिए लाती है उस शोख की नख़वत⁴, क्या रंग
उसकी हर बात पे हम, नामे-ख़ुदा कहते हैं

'वहशत'-ओ-'शेफ़ता'⁵ अब मरसिया कहवें, शायद
मर गया 'ग़ालिबे'—आशुफ़्ता नवा⁶ कहते हैं

Ki wafa hum se, to ghair usko zafa kehte hain
hoti aai hai, ki achhon ko bura kehte hain

Aaj hum apni pareshani-e-khatir unse
kehne jaate to hain, per dekhiye kya kehte hain

Agle waqton ke hain ye log, inhen kuchh ne kaho
jo mai-o-nagma ko, andoh ruba kehte hain

Dekhiye laati hai us shokh ki nakhvat, kya rung
uski her baat pe hum, naame-khuda kehte hain

Vehshat-o-shefta ab marsiya kehven shayad
mar gaya 'Ghalibe'—aashufta nava kehte hain

---

1. मनोव्यथा 2. सुरा तथा संगीत 3. दुखहारी 4. दर्प 5. ग़ालिब के समकालीन दो कवि
6. आकुल स्वर वाला

Her fealty is foul, our enemies say
To call the 'good', 'bad', has always the world's way

To apprise her of my plight, I go today
I'm going alright, but let me see what I say

O, leave them alone, they are of the ages of yore
They think music and wine can our sufferings cure

To what consequence her pride leads, let us see
At every word that my love speaks, I appeal for
God's mercy

'Wahshat' and 'Shefta' might write an elegy today
But Ghalib, the king of tragedy is dead, they say

है बस कि हर इक उनके इशारे में निशां और
करते हैं मुहब्बत, तो गुज़रता है गुमां और

या रब, वो न समझे हैं, न समझेंगे मिरी बात
दे और दिल उनको जो न दे मुझ को ज़ुबां और

तुम शहर में हो, तो हमें क्या ग़म, जब उठेंगे
ले आयेंगे बाज़ार से जाकर दिलो-जां और

लेता, न अगर दिल तुम्हें देता, कोई दम चैन
करता, जो न मरता कोई दिन, आहो-फुगां[1] और

हैं और भी दुनिया में सुखनवर[2] बहुत अच्छे
कहते हैं कि 'ग़ालिब' का है अन्दाज़े-बयां[3] और

Hai bas ki her ik unke ishaare mein nishan aur
karte hain muhabbat, to guzarta hai gumaan aur

Yaa rub, woh ne samjhe hain, ne samjhenge meri baat
de aur dil unko jo ne de mujh ko zubaan aur

Tum shahar mein ho, to hamein kya gum, jab uthenge
le aayenge bazaar se jaakar dilon-jaan aur

Leta, ne agar dil tumhen deta, koi dum chain
karta, jo ne marta koi din, aaho-phuga aur

Hain aur bhi duniya mein sukhanvar bahut achhe
kehte hain ki 'Ghalib' ka hai andaaze bayaan aur

---

1. ठंडी आहें और आर्तनाद, 2. कवि, 3. वर्णन शैली

130

Her gestures have a meaning all her own
So her love conveys something other than known

She has neither understood, O God, nor will she
understand what I say
If not another tongue to me, give her another heart,
I pray

You are in the town, so let you worry not a tiny mole
Whenever I want I'll go to market and buy a new
heart and soul

If I had not given my heart away to you, I would
have had some peace in store
If I had not died, I would have sighed a few days
more

There are other poets in the world, very good, well
known
But Ghalib, they say, has a way of expression all
his own

हरबां हो के बुलाओ मुझे, चाहो जिस वक़्त
मैं गया वक़्त नहीं हूँ, कि फिर आ भी न सकूँ

ज़ोफ़ में तान-ए-अग़यार' का शिकवा क्या है
बात कुछ सर तो नहीं है, कि उठा भी न सकूँ

ज़हर मिलता ही नहीं मुझको, सितमगर, वर्ना
क्या कसम है तिरे मिलने की, कि खा भी न सकूँ

Meharban ho ke bulao mujhe, chaho jis waqt
main gaya waqt nahin hoon, ki phir aa bhi ne sakoon

Jof mein taan-e-agyaar ka shikva kya hai
baat kuchh sir to nahin hai, ki utha bhi ne sakoon

Zahar milta he nahin mujhko, sitamgar, varna
kya kasam hai tirey milne kee, ki kha bhi ni sakoon

---

1. शत्रुओं का व्यंग्य

Call me with a little kindness whenever you like,
please try
I can always come because I am not like time gone-
by

Let me not complain of my adversary's taunt in this
state of frailty
It's not like my heavy head that I cannnot carry

I cannot procure poison, O cruel one, much as I try
Otherwise it is not a meeting with you that I can
not swear by

दहर में नक़्श-ए-वफ़ा, वज्ह-ए-तसल्ली न हुआ
है ये वो लफ़्ज़, कि शर्मिन्दा-ए-मअनी न हुआ

मैंने चाहा था कि अंदोह-ए-वफ़ा' से छूटूँ
वो सितमगर मिरे मिरने पे भी राज़ी न हुआ

हूँ तेरे वादा न करने में भी राज़ी कि कभी
गोश मिन्नत-कश-ए-गुलबाँग-ए-तसल्ली न हुआ

किससे महरूमी-ए-क़िस्मत की शिकायत कीजे
हमने चाहा था कि मर जायें, सो वो भी न हुआ

मर गया सदमा-ए-यक जुंबिश-ए-लब से 'ग़ालिब'
नातवानी* से हरीफ़-ए-दम-ए-ईसा न हुआ

Dehar mein naksh-e-wafa, vazh-e-tasalli ne hua
hai ye woh lafz, ki sharminda-e-meani ne hua

Maine chaha tha ki andoh-e-wafa se chhuntoon
woh sitamgar mire marne pe bhi raazi ne hua

Hoon terey wada ne karne mein bhi raazi ki kabhi
gosh minnat-kash-e-gulbang-e-tasalli ne hua

Kis se mehrumi-e-qismat ki shikayat keejay
humne chaha tha ki mar jayen, so woh bhi ne hua

Mar gaya sadma-e-yak-jumbish-e-lab se 'Ghalib'
naatvani se harif-e-dum-e-isaa ne hua

---

1. वफ़ा के रंज से 2. कमज़ोरी

Fidelity in this world is of little avail
It's a useless word, meaningless and pale

From the rigours of fealty in love, I thought, I would
be released
But even when I offered to die, she was not pleased

I am content even with your intention not to meet
So I never bothered very much to hear something
sweet

To whom do I go and against my ill-fate complain
How, I wish, I could die, but even that hope was
in vain

Ghalib died from a single slip of her lip, so frail was
his health
That he couldn't be revived even by Jesus' breath

कब से हूँ, क्या बताऊँ, जहाने ख़राब में
शबहा-ए-हिज्र' को भी रखूँ गर हिसाब में

ता फिर न इन्तिज़ार में नींद आए उम्र भर
आने का वादा कर गए, आए जो ख़्वाब में

क़ासिद के आते आते, ख़त इक और लिख रखूँ
मैं जानता हूँ, जो वो लिखेंगे जवाब में

मुझ तक कब, उनकी बज़्म में आता था दौरे-जाम
साक़ी ने कुछ मिला न दिया हो शराब में

'ग़ालिब' छुटी शराब, पर अब भी, कभी-कभी
पीता हूँ रोज़े-अब्रो-शबे-माहताब² में

Kab se hoon, kya bataun, jahane kharab mein
shabha-e-hizra ko bhi rakhoon gar hisaab mein

Ta phir ne intizaar mein nind aaye umre bhar
aane ka vaada kar gaye, aaye jo khawab mein

Qaasid ke aate aate, khat ik aur likh rakhoon
main janta hoon, jo woh likhenge jawab mein

Mujh tak kab, unki bazm mein aata tha dauray-jaam
saaqi ne kuchh mila ne diya ho sharaab mein

'Ghalib' chhuti sharaab, per ab bhi, kabhi-kabhi
peeta hoon roze-abro-shabe-mahtaab mein

---

1. जुदाई की रात 2. बारिश वाले दिन और चाँदनी रात में

How long I have been on this sorry planet, I cannot say
If I count all the nights of separation too, till today

So that I wait for her, and do not sleep all my life,
it seems
She promised to come when she came in my dreams

By the time the messenger comes back, let me keep
another letter ready
For, I know too well what her reply is going to be

Of the goblet coming to me in her mehfil, I cannot
think
I suspect, Saqi has mixed something in my drink

I have given up drinking Ghalib, but sometimes I
might
Drink on a cloudy day and a moonlit night

घर जब बना लिया तिरे दर पर, कहे बिग़ैर
जानेगा अब भी तू न मिरा घर कहे बिग़ैर

कहते हैं, जब रही न मुझे ताक़ते सुख़न
जानूं किसी के दिल की मैं क्योंकर, कहे बिग़ैर

काम उससे आ पड़ा है, कि जिसका जहान में
लेवे न कोई नाम, सितमगर कहे बिग़ैर

जी में ही कुछ नहीं है हमारे, वगरना हम
सर जाये या रहे, न रहें पर कहे बिग़ैर

छोड़ूँगा मैं न उस बुते काफ़िर का पूजना
छोड़े न ख़ल्क़ गो मुझे काफ़िर कहे बिग़ैर

हरचन्द हो मुशाहिद-ए-हक़' की गुफ़्तगू
बनती नहीं है, बादा-ओ-साग़र कहे बिग़ैर

बहरा हूं मैं, तो चाहिए दूना हो इल्तिफ़ात*
सुनता नहीं हूँ, बात, मुक़र्रर* कहे बिग़ैर

ग़ालिब', न कर हुज़ूर में तू बार-बार अर्ज़
ज़ाहिर है तेरा हाल सब उन पर कहे बिग़ैर

Ghar jab bana liya tirey dar per, kahe begair
janega ab bhi tu ne mira ghar kahe begair

Kehte hain, jab rahi ne mujhe taaqte sukhan
jaanu kisee ke dil ki main kyonkar, kahe begair

Kaam us se aa para hai, ki jiska jahan mein
leway ne koi naam, sitamgar kahe begair

Ji mein hi kuchh nahin hai hamare, vagarna hum
sir jaye ya rahe, ne rahen per kahe begair

Chhorunga main ne us butey kafir ka poojna
Chhore ne khalf go mujhe kafir kahe begair

Herchand ho mushahid-e-haq ki guftgoo
banti nahin hai, badaa-o-saagar kahe begair

Behra hun main, to chahiye doona ho iltifaat
sunta nahin hun, baat, muqarrar kahe begair

'Ghalib', ne kar huzoor mein tu baar-baar arz
zahir hai tera haal sub un per kahe begair

---

1. सत्य या परमात्मा का परीक्षण 2. कृपा 3. दुबारा

138

Now that I'm residing at your door-step without
                                    permission though
Can you still pretend that my address you do not
                                              know

Now that I have gone too weak to speak and mention
She says, unless I speak how would she know my
                                          intention

Alas, we are in the hands now of such a one
Who's known the world over as cruelty's own son

There is nothing in my heart worth speaking about
Otherwise whatever the consequences, I would speak
                                              out

I will not desist from worshipping the infidel born
Even if the whole world calls me an infidel in scorn

However much we may discourse on the true and
                                          divine
It'll be incomplete unless we bring in the cup and
                                          wine

Ghalib, don't you be repeatedly praying
She knows your intention even wihout saying